YOU AND YOUR PUPPY

in a nutshell

The essential guide to perfect puppy parenting, with easy-to-follow steps on how to choose, care for and train your new arrival

Carry Aylward

ISBN: 978-1-9161897-5-1

Front cover design by Nutshell Books
Front cover photo by TrainedPets
Book design by Nutshell Books
Photography: Cai Cheadle, Carry Aylward,
© AdobeStock, © Dreamstime

Printed by Kindle Direct Publishing

First printed 2020

Nutshell Books
3 Holmlea Road, Goring on Thames
RG8 9EX, United Kingdom
www.nutshell-books.com

*To you, the reader, to the adorable
puppy you choose, and to the special
times you will share*

CONTENTS

FOREWORD

So you're considering a puppy? Or your mind's made up and you're thinking, 'What next?' Or maybe you've already picked up your new bundle of puppiness? Wherever you are in this adventure, I am thrilled for you. Inviting a dog into your life, and especially a puppy, is hugely exciting. But it can be extremely daunting too. So whether you're new to owning a dog, or simply out of practice, congratulations on taking this step to being or becoming an excellent owner. You've chosen the perfect starter guide for puppy parents-to-be.

The first few months of your puppy's life are when he is growing and learning at his fastest – it really is the all-important formative time that shapes the dog he will grow into. What that means for you is that this is absolutely when you need to put the most energy into his upbringing and training.

But this vital stage also slips by surprisingly quickly, and there are lots and lots of simple pointers you shouldn't wait to discover only once you 'have the time'. That is the reason for this guide: to make this important information quickly and easily accessible.

This book brings together up-to-date research in a concise, easy-to-read and easy-to-navigate format to answer the most important puppy-care questions. Revealing only what you need to know, when you need to know it, it leads you step by step through the process, from deciding whether a puppy is right for you, to finding suitable options, and choosing your new family member. It then walks you through the preparations for picking up your puppy, the blinding brilliance of the first few days, and the turbulent trials of the early weeks and months.

For the sake of easy reading, your puppy is referred to as 'he'. But, for want of a better word, please consider 'he' to mean 'she or he' in every relevant instance.

If you haven't already brought your puppy home, then understand now that when the day arrives, your home life will become as giddyingly disorienting as a rollercoaster ride. Moments of pure exhilaration will be followed by fits of hair-pulling frustration. You will be showered with bucket-loads of love and laughter, and you will lose valued possessions and precious hours of sleep. There will be flashes of obedience and pure genius from your new family member, and then they will be matched with slip-up moments that have your head spinning with disbelief.

The advice in this book will help you manage these highs and lows, and build a solid foundation for a wonderful relationship with your dog. My hope is that it will keep you smiling through the love and cuddles as well as the puddles and poops; through the heart-wrenching nights and the shredded items of value.

After this mini exposé, if you're still ready to take this step into the pleasures and puddles of puppy parenthood, let's get started.

1. LOVE AND A GSOH

If you don't read another page, read this. This is the single most important thing you need to be a good and happy dog owner, with a well-behaved and happy dog.

Love

Love underpins the message of this entire book and the entirety of your relationship with your new family member. The love you have for him will guide your puppy-parenting decisions, actions and reactions, and, if it is unconditional – as it should be – it will make almost everything else in these pages feel like second-nature.

- You will instinctively have the selflessness, commitment, and dedication you'll need to take good care of him.

- You will naturally have the patience, tolerance, and forgiveness you'll need to cope with the more difficult times.
- You will have the inbuilt affection, empathy and kindness you'll need to quiet his fears.
- And you'll be equipped with the patience, understanding and perseverance that make all the difference when it comes to training.

GSOH

A fantastically useful add-on to this love is a great sense of humour (GSOH) – especially during the first few months. Let's say, for example, you discover that your wallet has been mutilated, your bank cards distributed and your cash notes shredded. The love you already have for your puppy will go a long way towards calming your reactions. But you'll find that a GSOH gives you perspective too, and takes you the rest of the way … to complete forgiveness.

REMEMBER: It's not what happens to you that matters. It's how you respond to it.

Of course, the wallet shouldn't have been left lying about and provoking your puppy to begin with, but we'll get to that soon enough. First there's some important puppy-suitability testing to be done.

2. ARE YOU READY?

Puppies aside for just a moment, are and your family truly ready for a dog? Any dog? Because in all seriousness being a dog owner is a momentous, life-changing and long-term decision.

If you are new to having a dog, you should understand now that your world will never be the same. You will start thinking differently about what you wear, the places you visit, your holiday destinations, the car you drive and, yes, even your next house. Your life will be noisier, messier and stinkier ... but also warmer, happier and richer in so many ways.

The dog you invite into your home should be treated like family. Ask yourself very honestly whether, at this time in your life, and for the next eight to fourteen years (depending on his life expectancy), you will be able to give him:
- the love,
- the time,
- the money,
- the space,
- the exercise,
- the care,
- the training
- and the patience
he needs and deserves?

Because **no** dog should ever be cast aside like a pair of shoes that's gone out of fashion.

Do you have other pets?

If you have other dogs or pets, consider carefully how a new dog would fit in to your household. A puppy, being both a baby and new to the family, shouldn't be too much of a problem with your other pets. Your other pets, however, might not be quite so adaptable.

Is a puppy right for you?

The puppy stage is filled with pooping, weeing and the chewing of everything in sight. On top of that, all puppies are energetic and demanding. They need a huge amount of training and socialising, for months, and in some cases even years. Ask yourself honestly whether you can face this, and whether you truly have the time and energy. If not, you might consider taking on a dog that has finished with toilet training, teething and even adolescence – perhaps from one of these options.

- An obvious alternative to a puppy is an adult rescue dog. It's not unusual for prospective dog owners to find a truly fabulous rescue dog.
- Another option – one that could save you a lot of time, money and hard work – is a much-loved and well-trained adult that simply needs rehoming.
- If you have your heart set on a specific breed, you could contact an established and reputable breeder to find out if you could give an ex-breeding dog the chance to live as a pet.
- Similarly, you could contact a guide dog association or related charity. Some really super

dogs that have been selected and trained for work as guide dogs or therapy dogs simply don't pass all the tests and come to need family homes instead.

If you value the quiet life, you should consider giving a home to a dog in its senior years. There are many beautiful older dogs that need re-homing through no fault of their own, so if you are no longer as active as you once were, this might be the best choice for you now. An older dog is likely to take longer to adjust than a puppy but, as long as he has been treated well, he will love you as his ever-own, no matter how old he is when he becomes yours.

Cost

Have you estimated the expense? Even after investing in your puppy (which could be eye-wateringly expensive), the cost of pet insurance, vets' bills, food, toys and care is no small consideration.

You still want a puppy?

I know. They're warm and cuddly and there's nothing as sweet as the pitter patter of puppy feet. But the first steps to getting a puppy really are a big investment – not just financially, but also in terms of time, energy and emotion. This is not an effort to put you off getting a dog. Quite the opposite. It's just really important that you are sure you are able to give your puppy the happy life it deserves, and **fully** understand the commitment you're making. Far too many dogs are re-homed and even put down each year because their owners underestimated the responsibility.

In a nutshell

If you're sure you can give your dog the love and attention he needs and deserves, and you're still sure a puppy is the way forward, then brace yourself for those four extra feet, and all they bring with them. And let's start considering your options.

3. WHAT SORT OF PUPPY IS RIGHT FOR YOU?

Dogs come in an overwhelming range of shapes and sizes, so you need to have a really good idea what you're looking for before you actually set out in search of your puppy.

This chapter will guide you through the most important practical considerations, and then help you to work through your own preferences, because what you want and what will actually work – for both you and your dog – are not necessarily the same thing.

Each question is followed by a handful of examples of breeds that typically fit the description.

PRACTICALITIES

1. How big will this puppy grow?

Too big? – If you live in a large house that opens onto farmland or a vast enclosed garden, then go ahead and choose a dog the size of a small pony. But if you live in a studio flat in a cold climate, then a big dog is a less-than-sensible choice.

Fitness and strength play their parts too. For example, if you struggle to hold on to a small but mischievous adult terrier, then a puppy from a large and powerfully-built breed will soon be pulling your arms out of their sockets.

Too small? – But that's not to say a small dog is always a safe bet, or even a sensible choice. If you've got small children who don't yet know their own strength, for example, you're probably better off with a breed that is physically more robust.

- **Large breed examples:** *Leonberger, Irish Wolfhound, Great Dane (above right)*
- **Small breed examples:** *Bichon Frise, Papillon, Toy Poodle, Chihuahua*

NOTE: Many of the particularly big or small breeds are prone to hereditary health issues, so before setting your heart on one of these, it's worth doing some extra research.

2. How much exercise can you give it?

Lots – If you're fit and planning on giving your adult dog a good two hours of exercise a day, then you'll find a wonderful companion among the more energetic breeds.

Not that much – If you live in a flat with no garden, can't spend more than an hour a day exercising your dog, and are planning on short walks around the block, then a high-energy dog would be as frustrated with you as you'd be with it, and you should rather be looking for a puppy that would be content with less exercise.

- **High-energy examples:** *Border Collie, Springer Spaniel, German Shepherd, Jack Russell. (Don't fall into the trap of thinking that just because a dog is small, it is also less energetic.)*
- **Less active examples:** *Bichon Frise, Yorkshire Terrier, Maltese*

3. How much mental stimulation and training can you give it?

All dogs love to learn new things and, just like their energy, their intelligence needs channelling. Mental stimulation and training are essential to keep them happy and well-balanced. In fact, they're essential for your mental wellbeing too, because if you don't or can't give your dog things to do, he is bound to find those things by himself – and the things he finds on his own might involve redecorating the furniture for instance.

- **Examples of breeds that need lots of mental stimulation:** *Corgi, most Collies, most Shepherds. These are usually breeds that come under the herding/ pastoral, gundog/sporting, or working groups. (We will look at these in the next chapter.)*

4. How important is trainability?

All dogs can be trained but, as the saying goes, some are more trainable than others, and a lot of prospective owners are looking for a dog that is quick to pick up and follow instructions.

The more trainable breeds are not necessarily more intelligent than other dogs, because trainability also depends on how co-operative they are, how focused, how keen they are to work and how eager to please. Characterful qualities like independence of mind and spirit by no means suggest a less intelligent dog, but they do make training more complicated.

- **Reputedly easy to train:** *Border Collie, Poodle, German Shepherd, Retriever (Labrador and Golden), Corgi, Papillon*

5. How important is affection?

If it's love and companionship you're after, some breeds are typically more generous with their affection than others.

- **Highly affectionate:** *Retriever (Labrador and Golden), Cavalier King Charles Spaniel, many of the Toy breeds (see Chapter 4)*

While almost all dogs will love their owners, if you have small children, other dogs and pets, or simply a lots of visitors, it is also important to consider breeds that are good mixers – easygoing, fun-loving and uncompetitive.

- **Good with small children:** *Labrador Retriever, Boxer, Staffordshire Bull Terrier*
- **Good with other dogs:** *Labrador Retriever, Cocker Spaniel, German Shepherd, Vizsla, Basset Hound*

- **Good with cats:** *Labrador Retriever, Beagle, Pomeranian, Australian Shepherd*
- **Good with other people:** *Labrador Retriever, Beagle, Bernese Mountain Dog, Old English Sheepdog*

Notably, the Labrador Retriever features in every category here, but only because it would be wrong to leave it off any of them. This breed is loving, good-natured, happy and optimistic, and it is with good reason that it tops the charts for the world's favourite dog, year after year.

6. How long will it live for?

The life expectancy of the average dog is 11-12 years, but some breeds only live to the age of six or seven, while others can comfortably reach 15. Smaller dogs are known to have longer lifespans than the larger breeds, and mixed breeds and crossbreeds typically live just over a year longer than pure breeds.

- **Short lifespan:** *Bulldog, Great Dane, Bernese Mountain Dog*
- **Long lifespan:** *Cairn Terrier, Jack Russell, Bearded Collie. (These dogs average 13-14 years)*

7. Are you happy with a pet, or are you looking for more?

Do you have expectations of your dog beyond being a loving and rewarding companion? For example, do you also want it for showing, breeding, as a working companion or as a disability assistant? If so, you will need to do in-depth research into the parents' natures, their abilities and their breeding.

If security plays a role for you, you will be looking for either a watch dog or a guard dog.

Is it a good watch dog? – Not to be confused with a guard dog, a watch dog sounds the alarm for anything unusual. It is alert, vigilant and loud, and can discriminate between regular goings-on and suspicious ones. It is not necessarily big, strong or vicious.

Is it a good guard dog? – Like good watch dogs, good guard dogs bark loudly to sound the alert, but they will also bark to send the intruder away. If their barking doesn't do the trick, they might move to Plan B and attack, but this does not mean they are aggressive as family dogs.

- **Good watch dogs:** *Terriers, Dachshunds, the guard dogs listed below*
- **Good guard dogs:** *Rottweiler, Doberman, German Shepherd*

8. How do you feel about grooming?

All dogs need occasional bathing and brushing, and some a lot more than others. Whether this is something you look forward to or something you'd prefer to keep to an absolute minimum, there are two main considerations here: coat type and shedding.

Coat type

There are lots of different coat types, but they are divided here by length, thickness and texture.

Length – It's safe to say that dogs with fast-growing, long and medium-length coats are the highest maintenance when it comes to grooming. Ideally these dogs need regular trimming as well as bathing and brushing.

○ **Examples:** *Afghan Hound, Bearded Collie (below: right), Cocker Spaniel*

Thickness – Dogs with thick coats and double coats usually don't need clipping, but they do need a lot of brushing. A double coat is a dense undercoat of short hair (which protects the dog from extreme temperatures), topped by a coat of longer hair (which repels moisture and dirt). The denser the undercoat, the fluffier the dog will be and the more grooming it will need.

○ **Examples:** *Akita, Chow Chow, Corgi, Pomeranian, Saint Bernard*

Texture – Dogs with rough and wiry coats generally need hand stripping approximately twice a year. This is a type of grooming that involves ridding the coat of dead hairs.

○ **Examples:** *Airedale Terrier, Border Terrier, Irish Wolfhound, Sealyham Terrier*

Shedding

Just because a dog has short coat, doesn't mean that it doesn't need brushing. All dogs shed (lose hair) to some extent, and many short-haired dogs are big shedders. Some dogs shed all year round and others, more considerately, do their main shedding over just two or three bursts a year. During these times you need to be brushing daily, if not twice daily, and that's just the dog. The floor, carpets and furniture will need their share of brushing too.

- **Some heavy shedders:** *Alaskan Husky, Golden Retriever, German Shepherd*
- **Some lighter shedders**: *Chihuahua, Greyhound, Labradoodle, Poodle, Vizsla, Whippet (pictured left: opposite page)*

9. Is it hypoallergenic?

Contrary to popular belief, it is not a dog's coat that aggravates people's allergies. It is the 'dander' that is found in their skin, saliva and urine. So if you suffer from allergies and asthma, and still want to share your life with a dog, then you should be looking at the breeds that produce very little by way of dander.

- **Good hypoallergenic breeds**: *Bedlington Terrier, Bichon Frise, Havanese, Maltese, Poodle, Shih Tzu*

PERSONAL PREFERENCES

1. Physical attributes

What sort of dogs do you look at with love, adoration, envy even? Which ones make you smile, melt your heart, blur your thinking and make your insides warm and fuzzy? Here are some questions, with sample examples, to guide you.

Shape – Do I like dogs that are slim and elegant (Whippet), big and cuddly (Bearded Collie), medium-sized and muscular (Staffordshire Bull Terrier), rough and ready (Border Terrier), or soft and pretty (Pomeranian)?

Coats – What type of coats make me want to reach out and stroke a dog? Are they short and sleek (Vizsla), long and woolly (Old English Sheepdog), long and silky (Afghan Hound), soft and tightly curled (Poodle), cute and scruffy (Miniature Schnauzer) or rough and wiry (Patterdale Terrier)?

Colour – Do I have a favourite colouring? There are so many to choose from. Do I prefer one flat colour (Black Labrador), or patches (Springer Spaniel), bi-colour (most German Shepherds), tri-colour (Beagle), brindle (Boxer) or spots (Dalmatian)?

2. Girl or boy?

Honestly, that's up to you. Unless you're hoping to use your dog for breeding someday, or planning on leaving him or her un-neutered, I don't believe there's much in it.

If un-neutered, females will come into heat every six months – which could result in mood swings and aggressiveness towards other females – and there is, of course, the risk of unwanted pregnancy. Un-neutered males could go in search of females, and lift their legs inside the house to mark their territory. (There is more on this in the chapter 'Going forward'.)

Neutering aside, there is a view that females can be more demanding of your affection and attention than males, while also being more independent and more territorial. And that males can be more affectionate, attentive to their owners and more exuberant, while also being more protective and possessive of their food and toys, and more motivated by food.

Use these generalisations as a guide if you like, but they really are dangerously sweeping. Males are slightly larger than females in both height and weight, but apart from that, every dog really is his or her own 'person'.

3. Weak strains or traits?

If you're opting for a purebred dog, or a mix that closely resembles one, is the breed you're considering prone to specific health issues? For example, it may be particularly susceptible to joint problems, or anxiety. The Kennel Club, thekennelclub.org.uk, publishes a Breed Watch list that ranks breeds by 'points of concern'. It's well worth looking up the breed you are considering, so that if it is prone to health issues, and you're not put off, you are at least aware of what they are, and can take the necessary steps to choose a puppy with the relevant health clearance. (See Chapter 6: 'Buying responsibly'.)

A decision for everyone

Unless you live alone, make sure you involve all members of the household in all these decisions. It's very important that everyone has bought into the whole idea from the very start. The more say the family has in choosing your dog, the more likely they will be to actively engage with and care for it, and the less likely they'll be to shirk their dog-walking, poo-picking responsibilities.

Bottom line

No matter what you choose, all puppies have the potential to be great dogs, and they all have the potential to be problem children too. Any dog kept locked up for long stretches, for example, will become 'difficult': barking, digging and chewing things. But if you can give your dog the love and attention he needs; keep him active and busy – mentally and physically; and give him playtime, toys and walks; you will have love, devotion and entertainment beyond measure, and big, warm paw-prints etched in your heart.

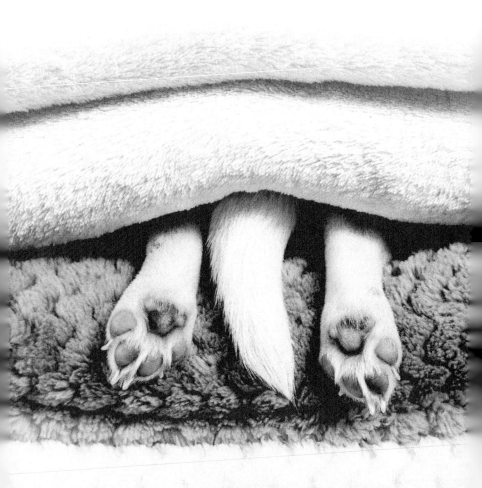

4. DOES BREED MATTER?

Choosing a dog is in no way like choosing a product, with set features, a pick 'n' mix of add-ons and however-many-year guarantees. Obviously. Dogs are as individual and unpredictable as people, each with their own unique characteristics, traits, thoughts and feelings. But that's not to say you shouldn't do your homework. A basic understanding of the breeds will increase your chances of finding a dog that is a really good fit with your lifestyle and family – and one that is likely to be as happy with you as you are with it.

Exactly how important your dog's specific breed line is to you is entirely personal, and it could be that you've already got your heart set on a particular strain. But even if you do, an understanding of the relevant breed or breeds' broader characteristics can still be helpful before making a final decision.

So where to start?

PUREBRED OR PURE MIX?

Perhaps the first question to ask yourself is whether you're after a purebred, a particular crossbreed or a mixed breed. To help with this decision, here is a quick definition of each, along with the key advantages and disadvantages.

Purebreds

These are dogs whose parents are both of the same breed.

Pros:

- If you take on a purebred puppy, you have a good idea how it will turn out by way of character traits and temperament.
- You know approximately how big it will grow.
- You usually know what sort of coat it will have.

Cons:

- Cost. The purchase price is usually high.
- Selective breeding can make them prone to hereditary diseases.

Crossbreeds

These dogs are a combination of two pure breeds, so the parent dogs should both be known to the breeder.

Pros:

- They are generally considered to be healthier than purebreds because of the larger gene pool.
- If the parents share similar size, features and/or traits, you will have a reasonably good idea of the adult dogs' size, looks and/or temperament.

Cons:

- They can be just as expensive as purebreds, and sometimes – with popular, 'designer' combinations – even more so.
- If the parents differ in size and don't share similar features and traits, then you will be left guessing as to the physical appearance and temperament of the adult dog.

Mixed breeds

A mixed breed dog is a mix of three or more breeds. These dogs are can be referred to as mutts, mongrels or Heinz specials – and sometimes with deep affection. But just as often the terms are derogatory, which is both harsh and unjustified, especially when you consider the many benefits.

Pros:
- With the advantage of genetic diversity, mixed breeds are usually healthier than purebreds.
- Studies show that they live on average a little over a year longer than comparable purebreds.
- They tend to be less expensive to buy.
- Each one is unique.

Cons:
- With puppies, it is difficult to predict the full-grown dog's shape and size, coat type and character traits. This might be just one point, but it is an important one. When you bring a mixed-breed puppy into your life, especially when the father is unknown, you have no real idea how it will turn out.

In a nutshell
- A wider gene pool generally means a healthier dog, that is less expensive at the outset.
- The more you can tell of your puppy's breeding, the more accurately you can gauge the adult dog.

BREED GROUPS

There are literally hundreds of dog breeds worldwide, but don't worry if you're new to this. As a starting point, this section will look at the breed groups. These are groups of breeds that share broadly defined characteristics.

If you're already considering a certain pure breed, then knowing what group that breed belongs to can be helpful in giving you a sense of your puppy's likely traits. If you are after a crossbreed, then you should consider the likelihood of traits from both parents' groups. Even with mixed breeds – which almost always have strong resemblances to a breed or two – it is well worth having a broad understanding of the groups they might be closest to.

If you've already got your puppy, an understanding of his group or closest groups will still be helpful in giving you a better insight into the instincts that drive his behaviour.

The official breed group names and categorisations differ slightly from country to country and kennel club to kennel club, so this is a nutshell simplification. It puts some popular breeds into six key groups, with typical traits and a few common examples.

Sporting Dogs / Gundogs
> *Examples: Spaniels, Retrievers, Setters, Pointers, Vizslas*

These are working dogs that were bred as companions and helpers to their sporting owners. They are energetic, with a strong instinct to retrieve game, and they make loving and loyal companions.

Herding / Pastoral Dogs

Examples: Collies, German Shepherds (pictured), Sheepdogs, Corgis

Bred to guard or herd livestock, they are lively, highly intelligent and love being presented with tasks and challenges. They make excellent family pets as long as they are given plenty of exercise as well as mental stimulation.

Hounds

Examples: Most dogs with '-hound' in the name, and also Whippets, Beagles, Dachshunds, Salukis

This group includes all breeds that instinctively want to hunt as a pack. Loving as they are, they are prone to wandering if they pick up a scent, or dashing off if something catches their attention. To prevent these behaviours, they need a lot of physical and mental activity.

Terriers

Examples: Most dogs with 'Terrier' in the name, including Cairn Terriers, Jack Russell Terriers and Soft Coated Wheaten Terriers

Small enough to fit down fox holes, and brave enough to take on their prey, terriers are feisty little dogs. Determined, excitable and mischievous, they can be challenging. That said, they are intelligent, loyal, loving, and a huge amount of fun.

Toys

Examples: Havanese, Chihuahuas, Pekingese, Yorkshire Terriers

Bred to be lap-sized and close companions, toy dogs are friendly, fun and thrive on love and attention. They can become very attached to one person, so it is especially important for them to meet plenty of other people and other dogs from an early age.

Working Dogs

Examples: Saint Bernards, Siberian Huskies, Mastiffs, Rottweilers, Giant Schnauzers

Typically large and strong, these dogs are built for strenuous exercise, and need a huge amount of it. They make wonderful family pets as long as they get this exercise, and are well trained with it.

FLAT-FACED DOGS

These are any dogs, across the various Breed Groups, with muzzles that seem to have been flattened, and lower jaws that jut out. The scientific term for them is Brachycephaly, and sought-after breeds include:

English Bulldogs, French Bulldogs, Boston Terriers, Pugs and Shih Tzus.

They have become very popular, and one theory for this is that their flat faces and forward-facing eyes make them appear more human than other breeds. Another opinion is that they tend not to need such long walks. But neither of these are reasons to celebrate.

While these dogs are lovely in themselves, have huge appeal and lively personalities, they are burdened with health problems.

- Brachycephalic dogs have breathing issues. Their airways are obstructed by the soft palate that is too long for the mouth, and their nostril openings are reduced.
- Protrusion of the eyeballs tends to cause eye problems.
- The short muzzle length reduces their ability to cool down, making them prone to heat stroke.
- Over-crowded teeth cause dental decay.
- As if that's not enough, they are often mistreated by other dogs who are usually friendly, but mistake their rasping breathing for hostile growling.

Please think twice before choosing a puppy from one of these good-natured but mis-formed breeds. As long as people keep buying them, breeders will keep breeding them.

If you **are** set on a flat-faced breed, ideally choose a rescue dog, or find a breeder who is selectively breeding dogs with longer muzzles.

5. LOOKING FOR YOUR PUPPY

By now, you should have a good idea what you're looking for, if not a pretty fixed plan.

In your mind's eye, there's the broad outline of a dog that's a perfect fit with you, your family, your household and your lifestyle.

But don't rush off to see the first litter you come across – even if you want no more from your dog than companionship. Why? Because it's close to impossible to resist the pleading eyes of a puppy that wants to go home with you. Once those eyes have found your heart, they are most likely stuck there for life.

Better to plan ahead. Start doing your research early so you can make a wise and informed choice.

TIMING

Once you have a clear idea of the sort of puppy you're looking for, the next thing to consider is the best time to bring him into your home and family. Dogs are sociable creatures and don't like being alone, so this should be at the beginning of a stretch when most of the family will be home and able to care for him full-time for most – if not all – of the day. If you are retired this might not be a consideration, but if you are a working family with school-going children, for example, you should try to pick your puppy up early in the school holidays.

The time of year is another consideration. If you live in a country where the summer and winter temperatures are very different, or the wet seasons are extreme, then getting your puppy at the start of a warm or dry season will make for much easier exercising and toilet training.

Serious breeders are likely to have taken these factors into consideration, so you will find that the most puppies are available at the start of summer and the long school holidays.

The next step then is to decide the date when it will be most convenient for you to take your puppy home. Good breeders won't let their puppies go to their new homes before they are eight weeks old, so work out eight weeks before your ideal date, and – unless you are already waiting for a specific female to have her puppies – that is when you can start looking out for brand new litters.

Ideally you want to visit the litter and meet the puppies around the six-week mark, if not before.

When to start looking
If you're looking for a family pet, your search should take no more than a few months.

However, if you're looking for a dog that is competition- or breeding-quality you can expect to be looking for anything up to two years before actually bringing your puppy home. It is likely you'll be in contact with a breeder before the litter is born, or even before the mother is mated.

PUREBREDS AND PEDIGREES

If your heart is set on a purebred you won't want to risk weak strains and traits, so it's well worth taking the time to track down a breeder whose puppies are a credit to the breed. Here are some things to understand and consider before you begin your search.

Purebreds – Many puppy farmers and backyard breeders mate their dogs with other breeds, and still advertise them as purebred. Although these puppies might grow into lovely dogs, they are unlikely to have the true traits of the breed you're after. Again this is up to you, but if you do want a purebred – meaning its parents are of the same breed – it is important that you meet the mother **and** the father. If it's not possible to meet the father, then you should ask to see photos of him, or even video footage.

Pedigrees – If you're after a pedigree – a purebred dog that is also registered with a recognised and reputable club or society such as the Kennel Club – you must choose a puppy from a breeder that has their assurance.

And if you are planning to show your dog or become a registered breeder yourself, you will certainly need to do more research. The section 'Useful Information' at the end of the book has a list of organisations and websites you can refer to.

A quality dog – The Kennel Clubs publish lists of ideal attributes for each breed known as the Breed Standard. This is what dogs entered into showing classes are measured against, and is possibly the best and quickest way to help you understand what a 'good' dog is according to your chosen breed.

WHERE TO LOOK

You can make a start by identifying the best way to find puppies for sale in your area.

Good people to ask:
- rescue centre personnel
- dog trainers
- dog behaviour experts
- vets
- groomers
- boarding kennels personnel
- members of breed clubs
- breeders at dog shows.

Good places to look for reputable breeders:
- the websites of the Kennel Club and breed clubs in your country
- dog shows.

This browsing stage will give you a sense of what the puppies look like when they are newborn and very young, and also of when puppies are advertised – some people advertise their litters very early, and some only when the puppies are almost ready to go to their new homes.

Advertising channels often feature males available for breeding, and if you see a male you particularly like you could ask the owner to keep you informed of new litters he has fathered.

Breeders range from excellent, to acceptable, to people who shouldn't be allowed to keep dogs at all, never mind use them for breeding. You might know someone who has beautiful puppies, ready now for their forever homes, and they might be the nicest people on earth, but that doesn't necessarily make them good or responsible breeders. And this brings us to 'Buying responsibly', which is arguably the most important and useful chapter in this book.

6. BUYING RESPONSIBLY

When you start looking for your puppy, you need to be super-cautious.

Whether you're turning to advertisements (online, in magazines or in newspapers), word-of-mouth or even friends, you want to be sure of two things:

1. that you are buying a healthy, happy puppy
2. that you are not unknowingly supporting the cruel puppy trade.

So before arranging to see any litter, always make sure it's with a responsible and reputable breeder, and not a money-grubbing puppy dealer.

This is how.

Dodging the dealers

Also referred to as puppy farmers, puppy dealers are people who breed puppies in awful conditions, then sell them from normal-looking homes which are, in reality, nothing more than a shop front. But dodging them is much easier said than done, because they can be extremely tricky to identify. If you're reading advertisements, try to read between the lines. These are some telltale signs that should make you think twice about a seller.

- Puppy farmers often use the same contact number on more than one advert. If the advert is posted on

the internet, do a search on the number see if it has been used on any other puppy adverts.
- They often use the same descriptions, word-for-word, in more than one advert. Search a key phrase in the wording to locate duplicate advertising.
- Photos of the puppies or the parents may also have been used on other adverts. Right click on the photo, then select 'search Google for image' to find out.
- A vet will not vaccinate a puppy before four weeks of age so if a person is advertising a vaccinated puppy that is three weeks old, stay away.
- Don't be fooled by promises of 'free puppy packs'. These don't necessarily make the sellers any more legitimate.
- If the breeder claims to be Kennel Club registered, check this with the Kennel Club.
- An inexperienced breeder might use the word 'thoroughbred' instead of 'purebred'.

The right price

Be wary of puppies priced well over the average, because silly money is unlikely to guarantee you a miracle dog.

That said, don't look for a bargain either. Well-cared-for puppies don't come cheap, and good breeders seldom make money from their efforts.

Making the call

When you're happy with the details given, it's time to make contact. You could do this by email to start with, and many people are more comfortable with that, but you will learn so much more by speaking to the breeder in person. These are some key questions to ask:

- Did you breed the puppies yourself?
  It's imperative that they did for many reasons, one being that you can meet the mother.
- Are the puppies currently in the place where they were bred?
  This should be a 'yes' and that is where you need to see the litter.
- How many puppies are, or were there, in the litter?
  It's always best to see the puppies together. Avoid seeing just one.
- Was the litter planned? And if not, do you know who sired the litter?
  If the puppies are advertised as purebred or crossbreeds, the breeder should be able to tell you about the father, and how he came to be chosen. With mixed breeds, this is not always the case but it's worth trying to find out whatever you can.
- Have the puppies had any health problems?
  Apart from being in general good health at the moment, you might want to know if there are any hereditary health problems that could affect breeding with a puppy going forward.
- How old is the mother? And is this her first litter?
  You really want to find out how many litters she has had because no bitch should have no more than three to four litters in her lifetime. These should never be before she has reached two years of age, or after the age of seven, and litters should be no closer together than one a year. A breeder that doesn't respect this is putting money above the wellbeing of the dog and should not be supported or encouraged.
- If this litter is not a one-off, what will happen to the mother when you've finished breeding with her?

Ideally she will stay part of an already loving home.

- Can I contact someone who already has one of your puppies for a reference?

   As long as this is not the breeder's first litter, they should be able to provide a contact.

- Have the puppies been treated for worms?

   They should have received at least one deworming treatment from the breeder before they go to their new homes.

- Have they been given their first vaccinations?

   Vaccination requirements vary from country to country, but initial vaccinations generally comprise two doses with an interval of two to four weeks. The first of these is usually given between four and eight weeks.

- Have they been microchipped?

   This is a tiny chip injected under your puppy's skin at the back of his neck. It holds his unique number which links to your contact details and, unlike a collar and tag, it stays there for life. If they have been microchipped that's a bonus, but it's not essential. See 'Visit the vet' in the chapter 'The first week'.

If the puppy you're looking for is a purebred, you should also ask these questions:

- Are you registered with the Kennel Club in your country, or a member of a breed club?

   Not all breeders are, but this is a good place to start. If they say they are, be sure to check yourself as well. Breeders approved by the American Kennel Club (AKC) or assured by the (UK) Kennel Club, for example, agree to certain welfare standards, to produce puppies in line with the breed standards, and also to reduce or eradicate genetic illnesses, usually joint and eye problems.

- Is it only this particular dog that you breed?
  Ideally, this should be 'yes'. Multi-breed breeders are often backyard breeders or puppy farmers.
- Will I be able to see the puppies' and parents' registration and pedigree certificates?
  If applicable, you should be able to see these, by email or on your first visit.
- Have the parents both been health screened?
  If the breed has any weak strains, they should have been screened for these where possible. There is more on this in the next section, 'The paperwork'. If the breeder doesn't believe in health testing, stay away.
- What health guarantees are you offering in terms of genetic illnesses?
  Because some health issues can be well documented, many breeders supply a guarantee with their pups that covers them against these problems. This will vary from breeder to breeder and the length of the guarantee will range from 12 weeks to a lifetime. A good breeder will give you some form of guarantee, and it will be written into the sales contract.

A good and responsible breeder:
- will happily answer all your questions on the phone.
- will ask questions of you too, to make sure their puppies are going to excellent homes.
- will keep the puppies in the home with the family, and not in kennels or outbuildings.
- will give you the impression of actively loving and nurturing each pup, as well as the mother, to make sure they are well socialised.

- will be happy to arrange a time for you to visit the puppies and their mother in the place where they were born and raised.
- will be happy for you to have more than one visit before pick-up if you feel you need it.
- might give you references of people who've bought puppies from them in the past.
- might offer to take the dog back if you can't keep it. Some breeders even include a contract requiring you to contact them first if you should ever need to give it up.

If the puppies are purebred, a good breeder:
- will be able to compare the parent dogs to the breed standard. If they don't know about the standard, or belittle it, you should stay away.
- will have photos and possibly video clips of the puppies' parents and relatives, and be happy to send you more by phone or email if you feel you need them (especially if a visit means a lengthy journey on your part).

A responsible breeder will NEVER:
- offer to deliver the puppy to you.
- offer to meet you at a random place.
- tell you the mother is out at the vets, or for any other reason. If she isn't there, the puppy most likely wasn't bred there, or there could be a problem with the mother.
- suggest that you breed your puppy for money.
- push you for payment.

NOTE: Never get a puppy if you have any doubts about the seller or breeder

Once you've found a litter of puppies you like the look and sound of, and you're as sure as you can be that they're healthy, happy and from a good home environment, set up your visit or visits.

The comfy blanket

Then find or buy a soft, comfortable blanket or cloth to take with you. This is so that, if you do reserve a puppy, you can leave it with him until you pick him up. It will absorb the smells of his mum and litter mates until then, and help to make the separation less stressful.

TIP: Let this comfy blanket absorb the smells of you, your house and your family before you go. Put it in the dirty laundry basket for a few hours. That should do the trick!

Then the countdown begins …

7. THE PAPERWORK

While you're waiting for your first visit is an excellent time to consider the inevitable paperwork. If you're looking at a mixed-breed or crossbreed litter, and the breeding is of little or no significance to you, then a lot of this next section won't apply and, in all likelihood, you can skip to: 'Vaccination and deworming records' and 'Microchipping details' at the end of the chapter.

However, if the puppies are purebred, or a very specific, popular crossbreed, such as a Cockapoo (Cocker Spaniel and Poodle), you should be asking for as much of this paperwork as possible.

If it can be sent electronically, you could ask to see it now, before the first visit. But if not you should still aim to see as much of it as you can when you are there. Ideally you want to have been shown or given most of these before you take your puppy home.

Parents' health certifications and ratings

Not all litters will have these – puppies from un-neutered family pets, for example, that have taken their owners by surprise. But all 'planned' litters should come with some certification, because the breeders should ideally have made sure both parent dogs were suitably healthy before mating them.

Even if you don't plan on breeding or competing with your full-grown dog someday, you should check the health clearance certificates and ratings for **both** parents wherever possible.

The importance of the different checks varies from breed to breed, but these are the most common tests for hereditary conditions, and a responsible breeder (particularly of a pure breed) will be able to show you the results from at least some of them.

- **Eyes** – Eye testing is almost always necessary to reduce the risk of cataracts and other eye illnesses in the litter. Ideally you want to see recent eye certificates for both parents – less than 12 months old – that show they are free of eye diseases. You are looking for OptiGen test results for prcd-PRA, and the results should be 'Clear'.

- **Hips** – Hip dysplasia is particularly common in the larger breeds – German Shepherds and Saint Bernards for example – but no dogs with hip problems should be used for breeding. The hip evaluation test gives a hip score between 0 and 106, and the lower the score the better. As a guide 0-4 is excellent; 5-10 is good; over 25 is unacceptable.

- **Heart** – Many dogs inherit heart defects so ideally the breeder should provide cardiac clearance certificates too, for both parents.

- **Thyroid** – Thyroid malfunction is especially common in many of the smaller breeds, but certain breeds – Poodles for example – always need thyroid clearance.

- **Elbows** – Elbow dysplasia is especially prevalent in some large, popular breeds, like Golden Retrievers and Labrador Retrievers. The elbow evaluation or elbow score ranges from 0-3, and again the lower the better. Ideally this should be 0 or 1.

For purebreds

- **Registration papers** – These are the certificates that record your dog's registration number. They also serve as proof of his pure ancestry, because to be registered with a legitimate registry, your dog must first have a pedigree. Ideally your dog's registration documents have been issued by a reputable registry, like your national Kennel Club, so beware of smaller, lesser-known registries which sometimes register dogs without proof of pure breeding.

- **Pedigree documents (where applicable)** – These show your puppy's family tree and list the breeding decisions that have been made. Pedigree papers are less official than the registration papers because a dog that is registered is always a pedigree, but a pedigree dog is not necessarily registered.

Health guarantees

If the breeder has promised a guarantee against any genetic illnesses, you should get confirmation of this at your first visit.

Proof of achievements

If the breeder has spoken of any competition achievements by the litter's parents and relatives, ask to see proof of this too.

Sales contract

You could also ask to see the outline of the sales contract to be signed by both parties on pick-up.

Vaccination and deworming records

You will need this paperwork to take to your own vet, as well as to any training classes your puppy might attend or kennels he might need to board at.

Microchipping details

If the puppies have been microchipped, you will need your puppy's individual number and the name of the provider so you can change the existing contact details to your own.

Unfortunately all certification can be subject to faking. On top of that, even the most glowing paperwork can't guarantee your dog's health or how it will turn out. And furthermore, there's no reason your dog shouldn't be a wonderful companion without any paperwork at all. BUT checking this paperwork is an excellent way to minimise the risk.

You've done your research and are as sure as you can be that the litter you've chosen is healthy, happy and responsibly bred. Now it's …

8. TIME TO CHOOSE

On the day of your visit, you'll be keen to get going, but before you set off, remember to take that soft, comfy blanket – ideally smelling of your house and family – to leave with the puppies in case you do decide to take one of them.

As soon as you arrive, you'll be itching to spend time with the puppies, I know, but first do the basic checks.

The owner/breeder

Look for signs of where the puppies are being raised. You want to be as sure as you can be that this is where they've grown up. If you suspect it is somewhere out of sight then you need to be super cautious.

Next, try to make sense of the puppies' environment. Is it warm, friendly and homely? Are they being brought up in the house? Are they in clean conditions?

Watch how the breeder interacts with the puppies too. Ideally they are being bought up right under foot and getting lots of human contact. Puppies that haven't had enough positive human interaction from six weeks of age until the time they go to their new homes can have personality issues for the rest of their lives. This time is out of your hands, so don't underestimate the importance of this check.

The mother

Look at her closely to see if she is the actual mother. (Sadly this does need checking!) Does she look like she's just had the litter? And does she interact with the puppies? Do the puppies' colours and features match with hers?

Once you're confident that this is the mother of the litter, it's well worth spending some time with her, and any other relatives too if possible, for an idea of temperament. They must be friendly and good-natured if that is what you hope for in your puppy. It's also important that they are confident, and not shy.

Another question is health. Does she seem healthy and happy?

The paperwork

Whatever documents you were promised before the visit, ask to see them now. And if you might be interested in showing or breeding going forward, you will need to scrutinise them for anything that could bar your dog from conformation classes, or prevent his or her puppies from being registered.

The puppies

Finally! Give yourself a moment to bask in the writhing bundle of furry, heart-melting cuddliness ... because frankly it's impossible not to. Then try to put your emotions aside and engage your thoughts for just a little longer.

You've met the mother and possibly the father and other relatives too. Looks-wise that is a good indicator of how the puppies will turn out, and presumably you're already happy with that. But now you need to study their temperaments and make sure they are:
- happy
- confident, friendly and interactive
- interested in you and everything around them
- energetic.

And make sure they look healthy:
- They should appear well-fed, with no ribs showing, but no pot-bellies either.
- Their noses should be clean, cool and damp.
- Their eyes should be clear and bright, with no tear staining or discharge. If a puppy blinks a lot, this could be the sign of a problem.
- Their ears should be clean and you can test their hearing by making a noise behind them to check their responses.

- Gums should be pale pink.
- There should be no irritation around the genitals or bottoms, or signs of diarrhoea.
- The coats should be clean and soft, with no signs of missing hair, or fleas or ticks.
- Movement should appear free and comfortable.

Which puppy?

All going well, you can finally let down your guard, and immerse yourself in the wonderful, overwhelming task of choosing. But which one? They will be as individual as people, so there are no right or wrong puppies, just ones that are more or less suited to you, your family, your lifestyle and your other pets.

Here are some tips that could help you with your decision:

- If you are absolutely sure you want a girl, you could ask the breeder to remove the boys while you meet the girls, or vice versa.
- Don't rush this. Sit down with the puppies and spend all the time you need with them. Play with them and watch them at play.
- See how they interact with you. If you play with one then turn away, does he follow you? If not, that is a sign that he is more independent than a puppy that does.
- See how they interact with their litter mates. Do they dominate? Do they walk away? Do they play nicely? This could be an indication of how easy they will be to socialise.
- Study their energy levels. Some will be more active than others and dogs with higher energy levels need more exercise.

- Sort out which ones are more submissive, and which more dominant. If you already have a dominant dog, a submissive puppy would be a sensible choice.
- Tell the breeder about your family make-up and circumstances and ask them for their opinion. They will have had plenty of time to get to know the individual pups.
- As a test, try placing the puppies on their backs and gently resting your hands on their chests. The puppies that struggle to get free are likely to be less patient than the ones that make little effort to get away. Another way to do this test is to gently lift them up off the floor, from a standing position and keeping them horizontal, just a foot or two and for

just a few seconds, to gauge how much they struggle.

- You could also throw something for them and see if they run after it, pick it up, or even bring it back.
- You could clap behind them to see if they flinch. Over-reaction could be a sign of a nervous disposition, while little to no reaction could indicate poor hearing.

It's often said that you don't choose your dog or puppy, it chooses you, and many people vouch for this. One puppy might spend your entire visit convincing you he's the one you want to take home.

But whichever pup you choose, when you've settled on your choice, that will be the best dog in the world, and time after time you will ask yourself how you got so lucky.

Before you leave

- **Money** – Assuming you're coming back for the puppy at a later date, the breeder will most likely ask for a deposit to secure your puppy. Make sure that you get a receipt and a written agreement that the contract is only binding if the puppy is in good health when you collect it.

  If the puppy is a purebred and there is no litter registration number as yet, the breeder should give you a signed bill of sale that includes reassurance that it will be available by the time of sale, along with the registered names and numbers of the puppy's parents.
- **Puppy contract** – Confirm with the breeder that they will have an official puppy contract ready at the time of collection. This should include the

health guarantee for the specified period (if one has been agreed); details of applicable health screening (for the pup and its parents); details of the parents (including their registered names and numbers); and all information to date on vaccinations, deworming, micro-chipping and veterinary visits.

- **Food and care** – Find out whatever you can about meals. What are the puppies being fed at the moment? How much and how often? Ask to see the food so you can be sure of giving him exactly what he is used to when you bring him home. Also ask about the extent to which he will have been socialised.

Finally, and still assuming you're coming back for the puppy at a later date, ask the breeder if you can leave your soft blanket with the litter so that when you pick him up, you will be able to bring all those familiar mummy-puppy smells with him into his new home.

9. PREPARING FOR THE BIG DAY

It almost goes without saying that when you pick up your bundle of joy, and destruction too, you will need buckets of love, patience, and that fantastically GSOH. But first, you will also need to have done a surprising amount of planning, puppy-proofing and purchasing of paraphernalia ...

Things to do

- Arrange a date to pick up your puppy. Eight to nine weeks old is an acceptable age, but don't pick him up before he is eight weeks. If you are travelling by car, it should be a day when at least one other person can accompany the driver.
- Book a visit to the vet for about two days after pick up.
- If you will be taking out pet insurance, do your homework now so you can have it in place as soon as you bring your puppy home.
- Puppy-proof your home:
  - Secure the property. This is the most important thing you can do to keep your dog safe. If you have a garden or yard, ensure the borders are escape-proof.
  - If there is a pool, pond or any deep or dangerous water he could fall into, fence it off.

- Check that there are no chemicals within reach (pesticides, weedkillers, fertilisers, etc).
- Cover or hide electricity cables and wires.
- Secure any unstable furniture such as book cases that could come crashing down.
- Remove sharp objects and small things he could choke on.
- Be aware of any plants in your house and garden that may be poisonous. It's worth checking online for a comprehensive list, but these are some of the more common varieties: Aloe Vera, Asparagus Fern, Azalea, Castor Bean, Corn Cockle, Crocus, Cyclamen, Daffodil, Holly Berry, Foxglove, Ivy (Hedera Helix), Jade (Crassula Ovata), Jerusalem Cherry, Jessamine, Hyacinth, Lily of the Valley, Milkweed, Mistletoe, Oleander, Philodendron, Rhododendron, Tulip, Water Hemlock.
- Remove valuables from the floor.
- Apply citronella or anti-chew to everything of great value that will be within his reach.

  (There's more on puppy-proofing in Chapter 13, 'New puppy safety' and Chapter 14, 'Danger alert!')

- Decide on his special place, a suitable comfy space that he can make his own. This is where his crate will be positioned if you choose to use one, or simply his basket and toys. Either way this special place should be somewhere central – somewhere that he can feel safe, but without feeling isolated or excluded. An ideal position would be against a wall in the room that most of you spend the most time in during the day.

Things to buy, make or borrow

- **Soft blanket** – ideally you will have left this with the litter when you chose your puppy.
- **A crate** (also commonly referred to as a cage, den or puppy pen) – this is optional of course, but it would serve as your puppy's own space, a special place where he can be safe, quiet and keep his toys. There is more about this in the next three chapters, but for now choose one that is at least big enough for your puppy's basket or bed, toys and bowls – and for him to stand up, turn around and lie down in when he has reached his full size. Wire cages are better ventilated than plastic ones, offer better views, and are easily collapsible for storage or transport.
- **Comfortable bed** – this could be a basket or a dog cushion, the mattress from a baby crib or even a folded blanket, as long as it is soft, comfortable and easily washable.
- **A collar** – choose one that is soft, lightweight and comfortable. He will soon outgrow it and you can choose a sturdier one then if that's what you prefer.

- **A dog tag** – no need for cow bells. Choose one that is small and light and have it engraved with his name and your contact details.
- **A harness** – harnesses offer little control over a large adult dog, but it's a good idea to have one of these for your puppy because they put no pressure on his throat when he is learning to walk on the lead. This should be a suitable size, adjustable, and comfortable.
- **Short lead (up to six feet long)** – again, nice and light. He's still little.
- **Extendable lead** – these can be dangerous and are not always permitted in parks and conservation areas. That said, used carefully and only once your puppy is used to the short lead, an extendable lead can make walks more enjoyable for you and your puppy.
- **Bowls** – go for a non-tip, non-slip design. Also consider a non-spill travel bowl for car trips, and a crate bowl that clips onto the door or side of your puppy's crate so that it can't be overturned. Remember your puppy will be fully grown before long, so consider whether to invest in big bowls from the outset, or get small bowls for now and upsize in time.
- **Food** – start with the food your puppy has been given at his breeders. After that you can move him on to the food of your choice. If you are concerned about making the best decision, consult your vet at his first check-up.
- **Treats** – you will need lots of these. They are fantastic motivators when your puppy is first learning the rules, and excellent for reinforcing

good behaviour. Choose treats that are suitable for puppies and avoid too many additives and preservatives, including sugar and salt. As a rough guide, the fewer ingredients the better.

- **A treat pouch** – a handy pocket for loose treats that keeps your own pockets from constantly smelling of dog food.
- **Chews** – your puppy will spend around four hours of each day munching on things, so it's up to you to provide what you want him to do his chewing on. Chews make a fabulous alternative to table legs and leather shoes, but with a young puppy avoid any chews that can splinter. Antler horns are good, and so are Kong toys filled with treats.
- **Toys** – he will need plenty of toys in all shapes, sizes, textures, colours and smells. He will chew on them, play with them and even snuggle up with them for hours. It's quite possible that he'll favour an old sock over an expensive toy, but can a puppy have too many toys? I think not. (It's wise to avoid giving him old shoes because, smart as he is, he's unlikely to differentiate between old and new when he slips inside your shoe closet.)
- **Anti-chew or citronella** – it's worth investing in either of these to spray onto those things he absolutely must not chew on. Expensive chair legs for example.
- **Poo(p) bags** – choose biodegradable ones to do your bit for the environment.
- **Wee mats/newspaper** – for housetraining
- **Pet stain and odour eliminator** – for carpets and fabric
- **Hot water bottle** – strong and covered

- **Grooming kit** – brush or glove suited to his coat type, and a dog shampoo
- **Dog seatbelt, pet carrier or dog guard** – if he is likely to travel by car.

Indoor extras

- **Baby gates/stair gates** – these are far better than closed doors for keeping a room off-limits. But stay away from stretch gates that he could get his head stuck in.
- **Exercise/play pen** – this is useful if you are leaving him for a couple of hours because it is big enough (usually about four feet by four feet) for him to sleep, play and poop in if necessary. This can also be an alternative to a crate.

Outdoor extras

- **Kennel** – if your puppy is likely to spend a lot of time outside when he is older, you should consider building or buying a doghouse. There's a vast range of luxury kennels on the market for you to choose from or replicate, but make sure the floor is raised. Other useful features are:
    - a removable side for cleaning (often the floor or door)
    - a doorway that keeps wind and rain out of the sleeping area. This could be a hanging rubber dog-flap, a patio space or overhang, or even a double doorway.
- **Kennel bedding** – any kennel will need its own soft bedding.
- **Outdoor water bowl** – large and tip-proof
- **Paddling pool** – if you live in a warm climate or

have hot summers, a children's paddling pool is great fun and a fabulous cooler.

Setting the rules

Before you bring your newest family member into your home, it's essential for you and the other existing members of the household to have a serious chat about the rules. Decide among yourselves where your puppy will be allowed, and when. Make sure you are all in agreement about which rooms and pieces of furniture are off-limit. And make sure everyone understands that sneaking the puppy into an off-limit area, or letting it break the rules in any other way, would only be unfair on the puppy in the long run.

Most families will agree that he is not to be allowed on your best furniture, which is sensible, but it doesn't mean you need to treat him like an underling. You can compromise by making sure he has a place he can call his own – a special bed placed next to the forbidden chair for example.

Choosing a name

You could choose this once your puppy is home, but either way his name is more important than you might think. You will be using his name several times a day for years to come so it must be something he will easily recognise.

- Animals respond better to shorter names – one-syllable names with a hard consonant or consonants like Tess or Zac for example, or two-syllable names such as Pop-py or Dy-son. You might love the name Penelope or Ophelia, but your dogs would thank you for calling them Pen or

Oophy instead.

- Make sure the name you choose doesn't sound too much like a commonly-used command: No, Sit, Down, Stay, Come, Here, Good or Fetch. Beau and Jo, for example, sound too much like No.
- And don't choose a name that sounds like that of another member of the household. If your mother is called Anne, don't call puppy Dan; if your cat is Tigger, don't call puppy Digger or Trigger.
- Choose a name that is easy to call out. 'M' and 'n' sounds are soft which makes them more difficult to call out loudly than harder consonants like 'p', 't' and 'z'. Molly, say, is a less effective pet name than Pippy.
- Never give any dog a name you wouldn't be happy calling out loud in public.

10. PICKING UP YOUR PUPPY

'Happiness is a warm puppy'
Charles M Schulz

The big day has finally arrived and there are wonderful, magical, hilarious, sock-nicking, poo-picking, finger-nipping, chin-licking times ahead. And more love than you could ever imagine. I'm thrilled for you.

If possible, pick him up early in the day so he can

spend lots of time in his new environment before facing his first night without his mother and litter mates.

Remember, if you are driving, to make sure someone is with you to comfort and hold him.

Before you go

- If you haven't already set up his special place in a safe but central spot, do that now. Crate or no crate, furnish it with the comfortable dog basket or bed, some toys, and also some treats if you like.
- And if you haven't already sprayed your most valued furniture with anti-chew, now's a very good time.

Things to take

- The remainder of the payment (if necessary)
- An absorbent mat (or similar protection) in case he relieves himself in the car
- Poo bags and cleaning cloths
- Two bowls (one for food and one for water)
- A small amount of food (in a container)
- A bottle of water
- A small selection of toys and chews
- A backup soft blanket or cushion is also a good idea (in case something has happened to the one you left with the breeder)
- A collar or harness and your short lead (not an extendable one).

The big moment

At last! Give your new family member and best friend a gargantuan cuddle, have a play and check that he's still in good health:

- happy, confident and curious,
- that there are no signs of mucus from the nose, bottom or genitals,
- and that his ears are clean and not smelly.

In the excitement

Apart from your new and perfect puppy, don't forget to come away with:
- the blanket you left, if you left one
- all relevant paperwork, which should always include:
  - a receipt of payment,
  - the vaccination certificate and deworming records,
  - his microchip number and provider details (so you can register him under your name and with his new address and contact details).

It's also worth double checking his food type (just in case it's changed), and finding out what times he has been having his meals.

And last but definitely not least, remember to thank the mother as well as the breeder for your beautiful puppy.

Travelling

Make sure your puppy is feeling safe and happy to be with you before you take him away for good. He is totally reliant on you now, so put yourself into those little paws that are being taken away from their mother and litter mates. Realise that he is leaving the only place he has ever known and, if you're driving home, he is getting into a car for the first time too! Ask yourself, "How would I be feeling now?" and "What would I need from this new person or family?" You'd want to feel safe and secure, loved and cherished.

It's advisable to put on his collar or harness before you set off. This is best done with two people so one of you can hold and distract him while the other puts it on. If you're using a collar, you don't want it too tight or too loose. You should just be able to put two fingers between the collar and the puppy's neck. If you've brought a harness, you should also be able to fit two fingers (and no more) between your puppy and the harness at any point.

If you're travelling by car, the puppy would be happiest being held by the passenger in the back seat. He would need to be held securely, so that the driver is not distracted, and be given love and constant reassurance on the journey. However, where you put him in the car will depend on the laws in your country, as holding him in the back seat could affect your insurance.

Your puppy will probably be too anxious for toys, but offer them anyway.

If the journey home is a long one, you'll need to attach the lead to his collar and stop every hour – more if you can. Like people, dogs can suffer from travel sickness, so it is possible he might be feeling a little ill or even be sick on the journey. He will also need these breaks for a walk and the chance to go to the toilet, but always keep him on the lead. Though he's unlikely to stray from you, it would be a terrible time for him to get loose.

At every break, offer him some of the food and water in the bowls you've brought along.

11. THE HOMECOMING

Give him a chance to wee before going inside.

Carry him into the house and put him near or in his special place, or his crate, with the door wide open. Sit beside him, arrange the blanket smelling of his mother and litter mates in his basket, and give him a treat.

Then let him explore his special place and the house, always staying by his side. Let him venture into all the areas he will be allowed to roam, so that he knows this is home. If there are areas of the house that will be off limits to him, then it is better not to let him in there from the start than to change the rules at some later stage.

Even if you intend for your puppy to be an outdoors dog, he should have access to at least one room at this stage, because he is not yet ready to be left outside on his own.

All the treats today should be given in his crate or special area – his very own bedroom. His comfy blanket should stay there and it is advisable to feed him there too. Do everything you can think of to make him feel that this is the best and safest place in the world. If there is a crate and the design is very open, cover it with a blanket leaving gaps he can see out of.

Puppies wee about once an hour and poop several times a day, so take him outside every hour if you can.

He will still piddle and poop in the house because he is so little, can't talk to you, and most likely has no idea that doing this inside is a no-no. Toilet training is covered in more detail later on, but for now be sure to clean up after him very well, and use an odour eliminator.

Your puppy needs 18-22 hours' sleep a day at this age, and today he is likely to need even more than that. But your presence is essential for his peace of mind so, when you're sitting quietly, let him sit with you and sleep on your lap or close by.

Make sure there is always fresh water available to him, and that he knows where it is. Feed him what he is used to and, as far as practical, at the times he is used to. At this age he is most probably on three or four evenly-spaced meals a day. Aim to give him his last meal of the day a good two hours before his bedtime, so he has a chance to go to the toilet before settling down for his first night.

12. THE FIRST NIGHT

Crunch time! He had his supper a couple of hours ago, and it's time for bed.

Take him outside for a last chance to go to the toilet. Stay with him in the place you'd most like him to go, and, be patient.

Back inside, make sure his crate or safe space is as appealing as possible, with his comfortable bed and his soft blanket. (In the short term, some people make this space in their own bedrooms, setting it up by the side of their beds. Considering the trauma of this first night, to your puppy and yourselves, there is a lot to be said for this. He still wouldn't be able to snuggle up the way he's used to, but at least he could see you and hear you and would know he's not alone.)

If his sleeping place is a metal crate, the openness still leaves your puppy quite exposed. So if you've chosen the crate option and haven't already done so, put a blanket over all or part of it, making sure he can always see out.

It's a good idea to make a warm, but not too warm, hot water bottle, and wrap it carefully into his comfy blanket. This is to replicate the body warmth of his mother and litter mates when they're snuggled up. Some people also put a ticking clock in the bed to mimic a heartbeat. And if the special place is not in your room, you could leave a radio playing softly to give him the sense he is not alone.

Scatter some toys and treats and make sure he has access to some clean water in his non-tip or clip-on bowl.

If the space is big enough for a place to relieve himself – aside from the bedding and bowls, then cover this with newspaper or an absorbent wee mat.

When crunch time comes, don't fuss over him. Just put him in his crate or special place with a treat, as though he's the luckiest puppy in the world, and close the door: be it a cage door, room door or baby gate.

In all likelihood he will cry at first, but he'll be warm, comfortable, fed and tired, so it shouldn't be for long.

Don't give him attention when he cries, because then he'll just keep on crying. If you do want to tell him he's a good dog, then first wait until he's settled down.

What about toilet time? If he is in your room, and you hear him shuffling around in the night, get up and take him outside. He won't want to wee in his crate or sleeping place if he can help it. (And it won't be long before he doesn't need this break at all.)

If he's not in your room, you'll need to set an alarm for the middle of the night so you can get up and take him outside. Alternatively, and only if you've laid down a wee mat, you could wait until very early the next morning. You'll need to do that for the next few weeks at least.

13. NEW PUPPY SAFETY

We touched on puppy-proofing in Chapter 9, 'Preparing for the big day', but as soon as your puppy is actually home with you, this needs another look – close inspection in fact – especially in terms of your own awareness.

People

The best way to keep your puppy safe is through your and your family's and housemates' own diligence.

* Be careful to keep doors closed and open where necessary, and don't shut them too quickly – your new 'shadow' could be right on your heels.
* Don't let your puppy play around cars or tackle the lawn mower.
* Don't leave dangerous objects or poisonous substances in his reach.
* Don't feed him 'people food' or let him get hold of it, and especially not chocolate!
* Don't let him near the edges of deep water, or high places: balconies, low window ledges, or unsecured staircases.
* Be careful with rocking or reclining chairs.
* Keep electrical cords well out of reach – apart from shock, he might pull something down on top of him (a heavy iron or boiling kettle for example).

If you want to be really proactive, put yourself in his paws for a moment. Being super careful not to underestimate his strength, speed or intelligence, get down on all fours and see what temptations call. Then take these away. Puppy-proof your home and make it as difficult as you can for him to get into any form of trouble.

Then watch over him, just as you would a busy toddler.

Small children

If you have small children, it is very important to supervise them when they are playing with your puppy. There is more on the subject later in the book, when your puppy will have become more boisterous, but small children must understand NOW that your puppy is NOT a toy.

- They must not be allowed to pick him up without adult supervision.
- They must not be allowed to disturb him if he is sleeping or has taken himself to a quiet place.
- They must not run around squealing, and if the puppy becomes over-excited they must calm down and keep still.
- They should be allowed to play calm games, but nothing involving wrestling or tugging.
- They should always stay on their feet while playing with the puppy. If children writhe on the ground with your puppy, he will treat them like his litter mates and mouth and bite.

Your other dogs (if you have them)

- Keep introductions short and sweet to start with, with your puppy on a lead to stop him from getting too close.
- If possible, let them meet for the first time away from home. Ideally, choose somewhere your older dog has

not been before so that the excitement of the new
environment will dilute the puppy's presence.

- Try to ensure the meeting place is somewhere no
  other dogs are likely to go (as your puppy will not
  be not protected by his vaccinations yet).
- Stand still or walk slowly when you let your puppy
  and your older dog meet, and try not to interfere.
- When you get home, if you have a garden, let the
  dogs meet there again in the same way before
  going inside. Let your puppy into the house first,
  before letting the older dog in.
- Lift any pre-existing dog toys and food bowls off
  the floor for a few days.
- If you are worried about your puppy's safety, use a
  baby gate or stair gate to separate the dogs in the
  short term, or put the puppy in his crate or a pen
  while the dogs get used to each other.
- Make sure all members of the family give the older
  dog more attention than usual.

Multiple dogs

If you already have more than one other dog, the
process is the same, but you should introduce the
puppy to one dog at a time.

Cats

When your puppy is this young, he is unlikely to be a
problem for your cat. But, to be on the safe side, care
should always be taken when he meets any other pets
or animals.

- Keep him on a lead when they first meet, and have
  a lovely puppy treat at the ready. If your cat
  responds by hissing and spitting to begin with,
  your puppy will most likely retreat. But if the cat

runs away, be ready to distract the puppy with the treat so he doesn't give chase.

- Always restrain him around the cat until he learns the cat is not something to be chased.
- Distract him with a toy or a game to teach him that playing with people is more fun than chasing the cat. Okay, it's debatable, but that's what we want him to think.
- If you need to keep your puppy and the cat separated while you are out, use the puppy pen or a stair gate.
- Make sure the cat has safe places high up that it can reach instead of having to run away.

Long-term safety

To prevent joint damage going forward, try to keep jumping on and off beds and up and down stairs to a minimum, especially if your puppy is allowed on the furniture. This is much easier said than done, but until he has stopped growing, jumping can put unnecessary pressure on his hips and elbows.

14. DANGER ALERT!

Non-edibles

Your puppy will be chewing everything now, it's what puppies do best – either because they are teething or because they are using their mouths to find out about the world around them. But there are some non-edibles it's particularly important to keep out of reach:

- Medication – human medication is the biggest cause of pet poisoning.
- Anti-freeze and other chemicals – many of these are sweet-tasting.
- Paint thinner
- Toothpaste
- Sponges
- Pesticides
- Household cleaners (including toilet cleaners)
- A surprisingly high number of household and garden plants can be poisonous when eaten in large amounts. (See the shortlist and advice in 'Preparing for the big day'.)
- Small metal objects like coins, and nuts and bolts
- Pins, needles and other sharp objects.

Edibles that are poisonous for dogs

It's always best to feed your puppy or dog actual puppy or dog food, and simply stay clear of treats from your own plate. But there are some foods that you must never let him get hold of never mind feed him because, while they are perfectly safe for human consumption, they are potentially fatal to dogs. These include:

- Chocolate (especially dark chocolate)
- Xylitol (artificial sweetener, commonly used in sweets and gum, but also in some sweet foods like low-calorie cake)
- Alcohol
- Onion
- Garlic
- Grapes or raisins
- Avocado

Also keep dogs away from

- Soft or cooked bones (especially from chicken or pork, as they can get stuck in your dog's throat)
- Macadamia nuts
- Fruit pips or seeds
- Potato peels or green potatoes
- Rhubarb leaves
- Baker's yeast or yeast dough
- Caffeine
- Mushrooms
- Persimmons
- Hops (generally in beer)

This is just a shortlist of some of the more common non-edibles and household foods you should keep away from your dog. It's not absolute, so it's worth keeping an eye out for fuller and newly published lists.

Swimming pools and deep water

Another clear danger is deep water. Never leave your puppy unsupervised by a pool, or anything deeper than a shallow puddle, until you are sure he knows how, and is more than able, to get out.

If you have a pool, it's important in the next few months to teach him where the shallowest step or exit is and how to get there. The best way to do this is to lift him into this part of the pool with you and show him how to jump out. If he is too small to jump out of the pool as it is, make a plan. You could place a few bricks on the shallowest step for example. Gradually he can learn to get back to the step (or exit point) from further away.

Some owners invest in a dog life jacket and teach their puppies how to swim right away, but unless there is real danger of falling in, it would be wise to wait until he is at least three to six months old (keeping him under strict supervision when near the pool).

Tying up

Absolutely not. Please don't ever tie your puppy out in the garden or yard, or on a trolley line. It's unthinkable that if you're reading this book you would consider this an option, but just in case, tying a dog up in the yard would make him frustrated, deeply unhappy and even neurotic. Sanity aside, it would put him at risk of hurting his neck or choking; prevent him from escaping from unpredictable danger, such as other dogs, fire or flooding; or simply from seeking shelter from fearful situations like loud bangs, or thunder and lightning.

15. THE FIRST WEEK

From just three weeks old your puppy has been socialising and learning to play with his mother and litter mates. Now suddenly he must learn to be with you, and with people, and to figure out a whole new set of rules. Luckily for you he is at his most impressionable during these early days, so the time and effort you put in now to building a positive relationship will be worth buckets of good behaviour over the months and years to come.

Mesmerisingly cute as he is, your gorgeous bundle of innocence needs to know his position in the household. He needs to understand straight away that you are the leader, and a strong one at that, or there will come a time when he is walking all over you and making the decisions.

We will look closely at behaviour and discipline in Chapter 18, but until you've read that, if he does something you don't want him to do, don't punish him or show aggression in any form. That would only confuse him and make him fearful of you.

Instead, distract him and encourage him into doing something good. Then reward him for listening. Encourage and reward – praise him at every opportunity for the good things he does in your eyes, so he can begin to learn what is right in your world.

Be clear and consistent in your praise and he will

become the most doting and loyal friend you could ever imagine.

Love him

Unconditionally. Do this and the rest will come naturally.

Teach him his name

Use his name to get his attention, and reward him when he responds to it. But be careful not to say it over and over again or he will quickly become de-sensitised to it.

Make his special place appealing

Associations with the crate or his special place must be positive, so it should never be used for punishment. Make it comfortable and leave toys and treats inside so that it always feels welcoming and homely.

Encourage him into this space and praise him when he uses it.

If he has soiled in it, be sure to clean it well.

Feed and water him

Your puppy should be having three (or maybe four) meals a day at this stage, ideally of the same food he was having with the other puppies in the litter. If you don't know how much to feed him, work out his daily allowance from the instructions on the food packaging. Split this allowance into three of four equal portions and work out a schedule for regular feeding, for example:

- Three feeds: 7am, 12.30pm and 6pm
- Four feeds: 7am, 11am, 3pm and 7pm.

(Make sure the last meal of the day is a good two hours before bedtime so that he's less likely to mess in the house during the night.)

If he's on dry puppy food, you can add a little warm

water and let it soak for a few minutes before feeding him. This makes it easier to eat and digest.

And if you have more than one dog, feeding them separately will prevent any possible food aggression.

Water should always be available. If it runs out he'll start looking for alternatives and you don't want him heading for the toilet bowl. Some large dogs can be great training for owners who don't keep the lid down.

And the water should be fresh. Don't cheat by just topping it up. Empty the bowl, scrub it clean and refill it every day.

> **REMINDER:** *Never let him get hold of anything listed in the previous chapter: 'Danger alert!'*

Manage toilet time

Remember that your puppy needs regular toilet breaks and it's up to you to help him with the when and where.

During the day, take him outside every hour if you can, and lead him to the spot you'd most like him to use. When he does it there, make sure he understands that was a good thing by making a HUGE fuss of him. Give him a treat and tell him what a brilliant, amazing, spectacular dog he is.

At night, he won't want to go to the toilet in his special place but when he is very little he can only hold on for so long, so ideally you should be getting up during the night to take him out, as well as early each morning.

"But what about when he does mess inside?" you ask. What of it? He's a baby. Clean up well and be extremely patient. No matter what you've heard or read until now, don't punish him. He won't understand. (There's a whole chapter on toilet training coming up soon.)

Visit the vet

Regulations vary from country to country, but take his vaccination certificate with you and your vet will advise you on what your puppy needs and when. Most vaccines require several rounds, between six weeks and 16 weeks, so scheme these in during this first visit.

Be sure to tell the vet if you have plans to take your puppy to puppy classes or boarding kennels, because either of these require further inoculation.

Get advice on deworming, and the prevention of parasites.

If your puppy has not already been microchipped, it's advisable to have that done now too.

If your puppy's baby nails are very long and catching on everything, you could ask the vet or a veterinary nurse to clip them for you, or to show you how to do it yourself.

Make the visit fun for your puppy by giving him praise and attention, staying by his side when he gets his shots, and telling him how good he is. Possibly take him for a walk or give him a treat afterwards to create a positive association.

Post-vaccination period

It takes up to two weeks for your puppy's vaccinations to take effect. This means you will need to keep him indoors, or at least at home, until two weeks after his first course of vaccinations, and also keep him from socialising with any animals that may not have been vaccinated.

Handle him

Your puppy needs to learn that he is safe with people, that they mean him no harm, and that he has no reason to fear them or react defensively.

He should start learning this straight away through lots of physical contact. Pet him and handle him: fondle his paws, move his legs, run your hand over his tail, feel his ears, touch his nose, gently examine his teeth, rub his tummy, groom him, bath him, pick him up and carry him around.

Play with him

Spend lots of time playing with him. And even now – in the post-vaccination days when he should stay inside your property – encourage him to experience the world through different surfaces. Put him on floor tiles, wood, carpet, grass, sand, rock, soft cushions, paper and blankets. Let him get used to them all.

Give him quiet time

He needs some time on his own too so he can learn not to be anxious later on when you aren't there or able to play with him. (See 'Time alone' in the next chapter.) Shut him in his special place for an hour, once or twice a day. If you have a garden or back yard, let him outside without you, or just with your other dogs, for ten minutes every now and then.

Loosen his collar

Check the fit of his collar every few days. He is growing fast and it'll need to be loosened regularly. Remember that you should be able to fit two fingers between the collar and his neck.

Insurance

If you're planning on taking out pet insurance, but haven't got round to it yet, do that now.

16. EIGHT TO ELEVEN WEEKS

FRAGILE! HANDLE WITH CARE

Your puppy is still weaning himself from his mother and you need to be ultra-sensitive to his feelings. Of course, you should always be sensitive to his feelings, but this is the worst time for anything to frighten him! From eight to approximately eleven or twelve weeks is the strongest bonding period with your puppy, so it's especially important that you give him lots of time and patience. But this is also known as the 'fear period'. It is a stage when puppies are over-sensitive and when negative stimuli are the most likely to leave a lasting impression. For example, a loud electric storm when your pup is all alone could lead to a lifelong fear of storms.

But this is also a time of opportunity. If he's already afraid of something, it's a good time to try to recondition him. For example, if he's afraid of umbrellas, show him that you are not afraid of them. Handle them gently in his presence without pressuring him in any way.

And from eight to eleven weeks is a particularly good time to show your puppy that most experiences are harmless. The more you expose him to the real world now, the more confidence he will have going forward.

SOCIALISATION

The best way to help your puppy adjust to his new life in your world is to socialise him when he still young. You will be able to teach him fancy dog tricks for years, but these next few weeks are the most important for getting him out and about. Use them well and don't let them slip by.

Socialising means introducing him to as many people and animals of all shapes, colours and sizes as possible. Visit friends and have friends to visit him. If puppy parties and puppy training are on offer in your area, take him along. (The chapter 'Stepping out' looks at how to do this safely and considerately.)

HABITUATION

He should also be exposed to as many new places and conditions as possible. In all fairness, you can't shut him indoors then expect him to behave normally around new people, places and things.

Take him with you everywhere you can and let him explore. Let him discover different smells, surfaces, sounds and sights. Take him into a park, to the school gates, for a walk along a river, go to a sports match, go to the shops, paddle through puddles. Walk him over and under bridges. Let him see cars and trucks and trains and planes. Thunder, lightning and snow might be hard to arrange, but ideally let him experience

different weather conditions too. Take him out at night and in the rain.

Feeling safe

It is imperative though that during these new experiences he feels safe as well as having fun. Helping him to feel at ease in new situations will go a long way towards helping him grow up to be a happy and well-adjusted dog, so stay with him through these new discoveries and don't let any of them frighten or over-excite him. Going forward, he can only be properly receptive to your training when he is feeling confident and secure. Here are some ideas to help with this.

- If you come across a potentially frightening situation – some big kids playing rough and tumble at the park for example – watch him closely for signs of discomfort. If he is hiding between your legs, or tucking his tail between his legs, you should back off and find a different route.
- Never put him under pressure to get close to anyone or anything.
- Be alert and sensitive to his feelings, so you will know when you can approach and when to stay away. There are many signs which mean different things in different contexts. (See the chapter 'Puppy-People Translator').
- If you are not sure how he feels, avoid having a tight lead, so he knows he has a choice. If he is curious, approach from a distance. Let him look, listen and smell, gradually closing the distance as he is comfortable.
- You might want to pick him up and let him watch from your arms, but always be there for him as a reassuring presence.

Accidental noise

Don't forget about background noises that you are accustomed to but that might well frighten your puppy.

TV, radio, internet and phones – Be especially alert during this time to the sights and sounds coming from your various devices. Dogs barking aggressively in a chase involving hounds, for example, could leave him terrified. Turn the sound down or off if he becomes alarmed – and before then if possible.

Tension in the house – Keep a good vibe in the house. If he hears angry voices or senses a bad mood, he won't understand that it has nothing to do with him (whether it does or not).

Fireworks and thunder – Close doors and windows, and muffle the sound with your own music or voices. Stay close to your puppy, showing him that you are not afraid.

TIME ALONE

Dogs owners are increasingly aware of their dogs' need to be socialised and exposed to everything, and many go to great lengths to arrange this exposure. But just as many owners forget that being alone is one of these experiences. In fact giving your puppy time alone is giving him one of his most essential life skills.

Puppies are social animals and don't like being alone, but most of them **have** to be alone at some time or another and the best way to minimise or even prevent separation anxiety at a later stage is to start leaving your puppy on his own now, just occasionally, during the day. If he is lucky enough to be right by your side for most of the time this is even more important. As with all his training, start practising this slowly.

- Choose a time when he is getting tired and likely to sleep soon.
- Take him outside for a little play and a toilet break.
- Shut him in his crate or special place with everything he needs.
- Ignore any whining and leave the room or go out for a short while.
- If he is very little and goes to sleep while you are out, open the crate door when you return so he can get out when he wakes.
- Start off with about ten minutes and build it up slowly to no more than an hour at this stage. For one thing, he will be needing the toilet.

BARKING

It's especially important not to punish barking between eight and eleven weeks of age for all the reasons we've considered. Your puppy should be allowed to explore and to express himself.

If he is barking because he is worried about something, and you know that fear is unfounded, lead him away from it and give him a treat. Reassure him with a gentle voice, then gradually expose him to whatever it is that he is afraid of, showing him that you are with him, that you are not afraid and that there is nothing to worry about.

AGGRESSION

Any dog can develop aggressive behaviour, and an excellent way to prevent this is by handling your puppy lots and often while he is very young. Teach him now that you can hold and touch him, his toys and his food whenever and however you please.

How?

By doing just that. Handle him, his toys and his food whenever and however you please. (Refer to the section on handling in the previous chapter.) That way he is less likely to become territorial and possessive over what he considers to be his things.

There is always a reason for aggression, and it is usually founded on fear and insecurity. But whatever the cause, it is unacceptable towards you and others.

SMALL CHILDREN

It is widely accepted that having a dog as a cherished member of the family is good for children's emotional development. But small children need to be taught how to behave around your puppy, and they must be supervised when they play with him.

Put yourself in your puppy's paws and imagine small children rolling around on the ground with you, giggling and shrieking, and how quickly that would encourage you to mouth and nip. Imagine being picked up continually, carried around, possibly even dropped, pestered, woken up. Think what it would be like not to be able to say, 'I don't want to play any more'. The only way your puppy or dog knows to tell someone they're hurting, tired, frightened or have had enough is to growl or snap. And the best way for you to manage this is to prevent it by making sure your puppy is not put in difficult or hurtful situations in the first place.

The following points are reiterated from the

chapter 'The homecoming' where we first talk about the importance of teaching small children that your puppy is NOT a toy.

- They should not be allowed to pick him up.
- They should not be allowed to disturb him if he is sleeping or has taken himself to a quiet place.
- They should not run around squealing, and if the puppy becomes over-excited they should be calm and still.
- They should be allowed to play calm games, but nothing involving wrestling or tugging.
- They should stay on their feet while playing, because if they writhe on the ground with the puppy, the puppy is likely to treat them like his litter mates and mouth and bite.

NOTE
If your puppy starts developing a habit of growling menacingly at you or your child, call in a dog behaviour expert.

FURTHER CRATE TRAINING

If you are using a crate and it started off at your bedside overnight, you should move it further from the bedroom – step by step if you like – to its permanent day-time position in the house. But only do this as your puppy grows in confidence and don't rush it. Your job is to build his trust.

If your puppy is going to be in the crate for a lengthy period while you are out, then you should leave him with some food as well as his water and toys.

FEEDING

When?

If your puppy had been on four feeds a day with the breeder, then by ten to twelve weeks you should be cutting this back to three times a day. Divide his daily food allowance (according to the instructions on the pack) into three portions instead of four and alter your schedule for regular feeding to, for example, 7am, 12.30pm and 6pm. And remember to avoid feeding too close to your bedtime, so he's less likely to mess in the house or his crate during the night.

Change of food

If you are changing your puppy's food, incorporate the new brand slowly. For example, for two to three days give him one quarter of the daily allowance of the new food with three quarters of the daily allowance of the old. A few days later make it half of one with half of the other, again for a few days, then increase the new food to three quarters and finally the full meal.

It's common for dogs to be hugely enthusiastic about a particular food the first few times they try it and then suddenly change their minds. Don't buy more than one bag at a time so that if he's lost interest in it by the end of the bag you can soon let him try another brand. Mealtimes will always be high-points in his day, so it's only right that you shop around for a food he loves.

There's a baffling array of dog food brands and flavours on the market, so if you're making this decision without the advice of the breeder or your vet, don't skimp – with dog food you generally get what you pay for. Make sure you choose a high-quality food that is appropriate for his age. This is because puppies and adolescents need higher levels of both protein and fat in their diets than adult dogs.

Although dogs prefer meat-based to plant-based foods, a balanced meal is one that combines both. If your puppy is letting off excessive gas or displaying signs of an allergy, you could try moving him to a low-grain or grain-free food.

Treats – You can supplement his diet with carefully chosen chews and treats, but avoid feeding him scraps from the table because, weight aside, this leads to begging and drooling.

REMINDER: Don't let him con you into giving him more food than his daily allowance.

COLLAR

Check daily that his collar is not getting too tight. He is growing fast and it'll need to be loosened regularly. Remember, you should be able to insert two fingers between the collar and his neck.

GROOMING

Brushing

All dogs shed to some extent, regardless of coat length and type.

Some dogs shed in bursts, and when they're in full-shedding mode they need frequent brushing – once or even twice a day. Then, in between these times, they truly don't need much at all. Once a week is usually enough, unless they've been rolling in something unpleasant.

Others dogs shed all year round, and if you've

chosen one of these and there's a part of your house you want to keep fur free, the only real way to achieve this is to keep that area totally off-limits.

The bottom line is that no matter how much, or how little, your puppy will shed, you **will** need to brush him, and **now** is the very best time to start. The good news is that brushing has lots of positives.

- Your puppy will grow to love it.
- It strengthens the bond between you.
- It keeps his skin healthy and helps you to pick up on any lumps, sores or parasites.
- It is very good for teaching him to be handled, especially during vet visits.
- Regular brushing cuts down on shedding, so if you've chosen a shedder, grooming daily during high-shedding phases will make a massive difference to the volume of hair in your house.

The less good news is that, at first, your puppy will have no idea what you're trying to do. He could take it as an invitation to play 'Let's eat the brush,' or he might be unsettled by the experience. Either way, he is unlikely to make this easy for you.

- To help your puppy get used to grooming, start with a brush with soft bristles. (When he is older and his coat is thicker you can use a stiffer brush – perhaps with fine, bent wires – for shedding the soft undercoat.)
- Have very short sessions in case he's getting restless.
- Keep in mind that it's normal for him to want to mouth the brush at first, so be patient with him. Soon he will come to cherish this time with you.

(See Chapter 4, Question 8 for more on coat types and shedding.)

Washing

Because your puppy's natural oils are keeping his skin and his coat healthy, you should avoid bathing him too often. (Even when he is older he shouldn't need more than four or five baths a year.) He does need to learn about baths while he is little though – especially if he is likely to grow into a large and heavy adult.

Indoor baths

- Use your own bath or a washtub. If you're using the bath, place a non-skid mat on the bottom.
- It's also advisable to put a strainer over the plug hole to prevent his hair from clogging up the drain.
- Use a quality dog shampoo, have towels at the ready, and wear old clothes and a GSOH, because you **will** get wet.
- Ease him into the bath or washtub, offering lots of praise and treats.

- Run a little luke-warm water from the tap or a hand-held sprayer and let him investigate.
- Working from his back paws, up and forward, soak him with the hand-held sprayer or a wet sponge, leaving his head till last.
- Rub in the shampoo and lather, then rinse several times, working the shampoo out with your hands.
- Finally wash his head, being very careful to avoid his ears, eyes and nose.
- Wrap him in a towel before he shakes too much, lift him out of the tub, and rub him down thoroughly.
- If you want to accelerate his drying, you could try getting him used to a hair dryer. Start a little at a time and blow in the direction of his coat. And NEVER use a dryer on a hot setting – always cool or slightly warm, and tested on yourself first.
- When his coat is almost but not completely dry, it's an excellent time to give him a good brush because a lot of hair will be loose from the wash.

Outdoor washes

On hot summer's days you might prefer to wash him outside. You will need a hosepipe and a clean surface that won't get muddy. You will most likely also need a helper to hold him for you. Either that or a space where he can't run off.

TIPS

Dilute the shampoo with water. This will make it go further and make it easier to work into a lather.

Holding a hand over the base of one ear will prevent him from shaking all over you. But step right back when you let go.

Nails

Whenever your puppy's nails get unmanageably long they will need clipping. You might well have had them done at his first vet visit, but eventually they will need clipping as often as every month or two, so it will pay off in the long run to buy your own clippers now and learn to do it yourself.

The sooner your puppy gets used to having his nails clipped the better. This is obviously not something you can practise every day, but what you can do to help him get used to the idea is to choose a time when he is already relaxed, then take hold of his paw and tap his nails gently with the clippers. When he responds calmly, praise him or give him a treat.

The next stage is to hold his paw and clasp a nail in the clippers – without making the clip but still showering him with praise when he stays calm.

When you are ready to make the cut, hold the nail so you can clearly see it from the side. Look for the part you can see through if you hold a light to his paw. This is because you want to avoid the 'quick' – the part inside the nail that you can't see through and that contains sensitive nerve endings. The whiter your puppy's nails, the easier it is to see the quick. So if the nails are dark and you can't see it, it's best to clip a tiny bit at a time, inspecting after each clip to make sure there is no bleeding.

If necessary, do no more than one or two nails at a time, praising him after each session, then making a note of the ones you've done. Eventually your puppy will be comfortable with the process.

If you want, you can file the nails smooth with an emery board.

Teeth

There are lots of treats on the market that double as dental chews to clean your puppy's teeth and keep his gums healthy. If you want to clean his teeth and to clean them by brushing, you can buy dog toothbrushes and meat-flavoured pastes.

TRAINING

Training is an ongoing, moment-by-moment process that starts the minute your puppy enters your life. It is all about the mutual understanding and clear communication that make life better for your puppy as well as everyone else in the family. This means that every member of the family and household should be involved, and should learn the same set of rules, spoken commands and body language right from day one.

The chapters 'Behaviour' and 'Training' cover the key DOs and DON'Ts to help you build a relationship based on understanding and respect.

PLAYTIME

This is not your puppy plus a pile of lovely toys. Playtime is social interaction, meaning you, or a member of the family, need to actually play with him. There's a full chapter devoted to this too, with key pointers to help you make every game and every play session a positive experience. The chapter also has ideas for toys and games, and it won't take long for you to figure out his favourites as well as the games you play best together.

EXERCISE

All dogs need exercise so they don't get bored, unruly, overweight or unhealthy, and as an adult, your dog will need an hour or two of exercise a day. But between eight and eleven weeks of age take your puppy on two to three walks a day of no more than 10-15 minutes at a time. As a rough guide, add five minutes to the length of each walk per month, so that by four months, he should ideally have walks of approximately 20 minutes each. As a rule, more shorter walks are better for puppies than fewer longer ones.

The chapters 'Stepping out' and 'Exercise' are both full of advice and tips for your outings.

Puppies grow up fast compared with human children.
One week in your puppy's life is equivalent to around
five months' development in a human child.

17. TWELVE WEEKS PLUS

Although at twelve weeks your puppy is still heavily dependent on you and ever so eager to please, he will start leaving your side to explore more. You will still be on his radar all the time, but you will begin to stop tripping over him whenever you step backwards.

His socialisation is still incredibly important and should be ongoing. As for chewing, he will be munching on everything.

Teething

By twelve weeks, your puppy's adult teeth, a full 42 of them, are waiting to push out those super-sharp baby teeth. He will start chewing on everything and his gums will be sore and swollen. It will then take until around 18 weeks for those baby teeth to even start falling out. That's a lot of weeks of important chewing to be done so – for the sake of your puppy, your house and your sanity – keep valuables out of reach, and always have an abundant and ready supply of toys and treats that he is allowed to chew on.

TIP
Tie a knot in an old cloth, wet it and put it in the freezer. Then give it to him when it is frozen to ease his sore gums

Sleep

By this age, your puppy no longer needs the 18-22 hours' sleep he needed when you brought him home, but he does still need a good 16 hours of rest or sleep a day.

Food

- **Twelve weeks to five months:** For now, keep to three feeds a day. And remember not to feed him too close to your bedtime.
- **Five months to a year:** By five months you can gradually bring the meals down to twice a day, which is how often he will need feeding as an adult dog.

If your puppy is not faring well on commercially produced food, you could try putting him on a raw diet, which is home-prepared food with an emphasis on raw meat, whole or crushed bones, vegetables, fruits, raw eggs and some dairy. There is a lot of controversy around the subject of raw diets, so if you are considering this route, you will need to research the subject thoroughly.

The following chapters (right up to 'Puppy-People Translator') focus on the most important and pressing puppy issues in terms of behaviour and training, and are filled with tips to help you as you guide your little one into adolescence and beyond.

18. BEHAVIOUR

Your puppy loves you so much. He wants to learn from you and please you. But he only knows what his survival instincts tell him, so, to reiterate, it's your job to teach him what is and isn't allowed in your world.

We will look at specific behaviours in the next chapters, but the pointers in this general chapter are fundamental to all of these.

For a well-behaved puppy, the first thing to understand – as you surely do by now – is that puppies are much more receptive when they have nothing to fear. A fearful puppy will never be totally engaged.

Our understanding of animal behaviour is improving all the time, and it's no longer acceptable to punish dogs, never mind puppies, by shouting, smacking and rubbing their noses in the carpet. This sort of treatment is both ineffective and counterproductive. It scares your puppy and puts you in a bad mood. You lose your dog's trust and the spinout of that – into all the other areas of the relationship – is just not worth thinking about. You want your puppy to be happy and optimistic, looking forward to everything, rather than fearing it.

So how do you achieve this? In a nutshell: you gain his trust by focusing on the things he does right. By encouraging good behaviour and rewarding it!

Encourage and reward

Always tell him what you DO want him to do, rather than what you DON'T want him to do. Let's say for example he's got the TV remote between his teeth. Don't shout and get angry. Calmly distract him with something else, something he IS allowed to chew on. Refocus him on this new and exciting toy, and rescue the remote. If you don't have anything at hand, then ask him to do something to obey you – even something as simple as a 'Sit!'

His feelings are everything

Let's say your puppy bounds up to you with a glint in his eye, a wag in his tail and a captured, dishevelled bathmat in his mouth. Try not to think about your favourite bathmat which, after all, is just a thing and has no feelings at all. Instead, think about HOW HE'S FEELING about what he's done. He thinks he's done brilliantly, doesn't he? He wants a medal. Scold him now and you'll really confuse him. Then again, if you praise him, he might keep bringing you bathmat-type presents ad infinitum. So what do you do?

You don't scold or praise. Distract him instead by calling him to you and getting his attention onto something else, a toy perhaps. When he is refocused on the toy, offer him a tempting chew. By then the bathmat should be far from his mind, and you should be able to rescue it. And if it's still functional, remember to hang it up out of his puppy-jaw reach for a few months.

You are the leader

To establish a positive relationship, your puppy must understand from the start that, even though you love him and you are best friends, your word is law and he must listen to you. And he will, as long as you are a worthy leader and a good teacher.

Here are some key tips for you.

- Don't be aggressive towards him. Instead, be gentle but firm.
- Don't go too easy on him either. In the long run that can be as unfair as punishing him.
- Be crystal clear in your instructions. Use single words rather than sentences and try to be consistent in your choice of words. Don't switch between 'Come!' and 'Here!' for example, or 'Walk!' and 'Heel!'.
- Keep your tone positive.
- Use body language as well as verbal commands.
- When he does what you want, show him unreservedly how clever he is. Be happy and excited and reward him with praise.

Timing is all-important

It's vital that you teach your puppy with timely signals – signals that apply to what he is doing AT THAT TIME. If you discipline him for something he did two minutes ago, he won't understand the reason. For example, if he runs off after a cat and then comes back, and you shout at him for chasing the cat as he is coming back, he will naturally think you are shouting at him for coming back and not for chasing the cat. The result? He is confused and intimidated, and next time he will think twice about coming back. Too many well-meaning dog owners make the mistake of misplaced timing – and it's simply unfair.

Prevent bad behaviour

- Try to anticipate things that might go wrong. If you think he's about to chase the cat, hold on to him and distract him with a toy. Billowing tablecloths, for example, are begging for trouble. Don't use them until he's older.
- Make sure his basic needs are met: love, food, water, warmth, things to chew on, sleep, play, exercise and exploration. If he has all of these he is far less likely to behave badly in the first place.
- Don't put temptation in his way. If you don't want him eating from your dinner plate, don't leave it lying around, unattended and in easy reach. That would just be setting him up to fail.

Let him know when you disapprove

In many bad behaviours, the best way to tell your puppy you don't like what he's doing is to take away something he wants – your attention. Discourage bad behaviour by ignoring him when he is behaving in any way that is not acceptable to you. Stop play, walk away, look away, leave the room if you can.

When to say 'No!' or 'Leave!'

1. When your puppy does something totally unacceptable, something that could endanger his life for example.

2. When he boldly ignores your voice command because he would rather do something else.

These need to be corrected immediately and here's how.

- Reprimand him straight away. Say 'NO!' or 'LEAVE!' in a voice that is loud and startling enough to prevent or stop his behaviour. It should be in stark contrast to your usual quiet and calm voice, and used sparingly for best effect.
- Block his way with your body, or physically stop him if you need to.
- Then make eye contact and use your voice to get him to focus on you.
- Once you have his attention, praise him for changing his focus.
- The trouble with 'No' and 'Leave' is that your puppy doesn't know what he's meant to do instead. Always try to give him something better to do or to chew on.

Still struggling?

If you've tried all these things with a bad behaviour, with repeated, clear and consistent communication, and you're still struggling, you can resort to time-out. Shut him in the kitchen, or a similar and safe place, and leave him for a few minutes – five is acceptable, ten is too long.

Alternatively, you can tie him up in a safe and suitable time-out spot, and ignore him for five minutes. (Never go out and leave him like that.) The lead should be just long enough for him to be able to sit up and lie down comfortably.

Rules must be consistent

We've been here before, but this is really important. If one person lets your puppy onto the sofa, it's downright unfair for someone else to reprimand him for being there.

Rules will be very confusing if they differ from person to person, so it's really crucial that everyone in your puppy's life understands and teaches what is and what isn't allowed in precisely the same way.

TIP
Write a list of puppy rules, and post it around the house, because before you know it, you will be trying to remember what you agreed

Serious behavioural problems

Here it is especially important that you are able to tell the difference between playfulness and aggression. See the chapter 'Puppy-People Translator' for clues on reading the signs. If your puppy develops any traits that could endanger you, himself, or any other person or their dog, you should immediately get help from a professional in dog behaviour.

Serious issues range from biting, growling and any form of aggression towards people or other dogs to problems as simple as jumping up, which, although meant as a show of affection, can easily cause injury. But less dangerous issues – like incessant barking, nipping, constantly demanding attention, chewing on everything, and even relieving themselves inside the house – can become increasingly troublesome too. All of these are caused by something, and common reasons include boredom, loneliness, lack of socialisation, lack of training, fear, anxiety or insecurity, being spoilt and having been badly treated.

It's far more difficult to manage existing behavioural problems than it is to prevent them from developing at the outset. So the first thing you can actively do to ensure a happy and well-behaved puppy is to buy from a loving and responsible breeder. The first eight or so weeks of his life were out of your hands, so choosing responsibly is an excellent first step to minimising the risk of early trauma.

The next step, once he's home with you, is to **not** give him reason to develop behavioural issues. Let's look in some detail at how to nip them in the bud while he's at his most impressionable.

19. JUMPING UP

Your puppy will jump up at you: because he is happy to see you, because he loves you, because he wants to lick you all over your face and he can't reach, because he wants you to pet him and play with him. With his mother and litter mates this was quite normal, but now he needs to learn that with people it's not okay.

It's possible you don't mind him jumping up right now – after all he is not likely to bowl anyone over with his loving greetings while he is little – but if he's going to grow into a heavy adult he could easily send someone flying.

That's not to say jumping up doesn't matter if your puppy will always be little, because, size aside, all dogs are prone to muddy paws and sharp claws.

Basically, jumping up soon becomes a nuisance, and you want to nip it in the bud before it gets out of hand. This is how to respond when he tries to jump up, and the sooner you start, the better.

Do
- Step back so that his paws don't reach you
- Look away from him
- Turn away from him
- Lift your hands away and don't touch him
- After a few seconds, come back to him, and repeat if necessary

- When he has
  quietened
  down and
  stopped
  jumping, be
  sure to praise
  him and reward
  him.
- Get all family
  members to do this,
  and ask regular visitors
  to help with this too.
- If jumping up on
  visitors is likely, put
  him on a lead
  before opening
  the door to them.

Don't

- Reward him
- Talk to him
- Tell him to get down
- Push him away
- Shout or yell
- Smack him or use
  physical punishment of
  any sort.

How does it work?

By repeating these responses, he will come to realise
that if he keeps his four paws on the ground he will be
rewarded with praise and the attention he is looking
for, and that if he jumps up he will be ignored.

20. TOILET TRAINING

Remember, at first your puppy has no idea that the house is not a public toilet. This is something you need to teach him and it will take time and patience.

Initially, take him outside hourly and show him where to go. When he does go in an acceptable place, and as soon as he has finished his business, it's time to celebrate. Reward! Reward! Reward! That way you will teach him that doing his business outside means AMAZING things will happen.

Here are some key DOs and DON'Ts to help speed up the process.

Do

- When your puppy arrives at your house for the first time, give him a guided tour. The sooner he understands that all this space is living area, the sooner he will stop using it as a toilet.
- Take him outside every hour.
- Also take him outside immediately if you spot any of these tell-tale signs:
  ◦ Sniffing and circling the floor
  ◦ Whining
  ◦ Pacing up and down
  ◦ Scratching the floor.
- Lead him to the spot you'd like to encourage him to use.

- Then wait. And wait some more. Stay out there with him – come rain or shine – watching him all the time.
- You can spur him on with an encouraging command, like 'quickly now' or 'piddle time'.
- Wait until he's completely finished before you reward him, or he might only do half his business.
- As soon as he is finished, shower him with praise.
- When he goes to the toilet inside, thoroughly clean the area he's marked, finishing with a pet-safe odour eliminator. This is important because he is most likely to do his business in a place where he can already smell traces of a previous piddle or poop.
- One of the best ways to teach him not to mess inside is to keep your house clean and free of smells. If possible, put a limit on his access to carpeted areas that are difficult to clean well.
- If he has messed inside but on a training mat or piece of newspaper, carry this outside to where you'd ideally like him to go, and weigh it down there with a stone so it can't blow away. The smell will act as a signal for to him to do his business there in future.

Don't
- Punish him for piddling or pooping inside. Punishing him for something he can't help and doesn't fully understand would only make him nervous and slow his progress.
- Leave him outside on his own. He will just turn his attention to getting back to you, and when he does get back inside the house, he will very likely still need to go.

How long will toilet training take?

Progress obviously varies from puppy to puppy, but it's safe to assume he will leave the odd surprise for you until he's around six months of age, and it could take up to a year for him to be accident free. Be patient.

NOTES

Your puppy will never wee or poop to spite you.

———

Some dogs make a little wee as a sign of submission, and some wee with excitement. These lapses should never be punished!

TIP

Once your puppy understands that you want him to do his toiletries outside, you can hang a bell on a string from the door that leads out. He might well learn to jingle the bell to tell you when he needs to go.

21. MOUTHING AND NIPPING

All dogs love to play, and play involves mouthing one another, so it's natural for your puppy to want to play bite. He might also bite because he is teething. If, like many new puppy owners, you don't mind your puppy chewing your hands at this stage, you soon will, because as he gets older, the biting will get harder and involve others too. He should learn as soon as possible not to use his teeth on people.

Adult dogs are good at controlling the pressure of their jaws, but puppies are still learning and practising jaw control, and often make the mistake of biting too hard. When your puppy bit one of his litter mates too hard while playing, the hurt puppy would have yelped and stopped playing. So your puppy has already learned that biting too hard puts a damper on play time. He will learn gradually to play more gently until he understands not to let his teeth into contact with your skin at all.

Do

- Play with him with a chew toy in your hand. If he bites you and inflicts pain, make a high yelping sound and immediately withdraw your hand. This is exactly what would have happened with his litter mates, so it will help him to learn that it's okay to nip the chew toy, but not your hand.

- If the biting persists, remove yourself from the game, the room even, just for a few minutes to show him that teeth on skin equals no more playing. It's not a quick fix, but he will gradually make the association.
- Supervise small children. Their tendency when a puppy mouths them is to scream and run around, which only excites and encourages the puppy even more.

Don't

- Shout at him or smack him if he mouths or nips. This can make the biting harder to control.
- Rush him. He must learn jaw control gradually and through experience.
- Play rough tug games – they just encourage biting.

22. CHEWING HOUSE AND HOME

*'Puppies are constantly inventing new ways to
be bad. It's fascinating. You come into a room
they've been in and see pieces of debris and try
to figure out what you had that was made from
wicker or what had been stuffed with fluff'*
Julie Klam

All dogs chew, especially puppies. They chew things
either because they are teething or simply to explore.
Chewing is how they learn about the world around
them – they don't have hands, so they inspect
everything they can with their mouths and teeth.

Your puppy will chew on anything he can reach, so
it's really important to give him things you are happy
for him to chew on.

Don't

- leave valuable and tempting chewables, like shoes,
  lying around on the floor.
- leave supposedly-less-tempting items lying around
  either: spectacles, sunglasses, mobile phones, car
  keys … Puppies are excellent training for untidy
  owners.
- encourage sticks. They can splinter and get stuck in
  his mouth.
- try to wrench a forbidden item from his jaws. It's

not unusual for puppies to swallow the item instead of giving it up.
- start a tug-of-war.

Do

- Instead of trying to pull or coax a non-chew item from your puppy, replace it with something he is allowed to chew on – and make sure this replacement offering is something you know he loves. As he plays with the forbidden item, hold the new and better offering to his nose and say, 'Leave!', 'Drop!' or 'Off!'
- When he drops it, you can give him the treat and a pat.
- Make sure you have lots of puppy toys and treats. (Pet toys are created to appeal to your dog by smell, taste, feel and shape, but you can also use old soft toys.)
- Keep these tempting prizes close by. You never know when you'll be needing them, but if you assume it's always you won't be caught out.
- If you see your puppy approaching something with demolition on his mind, call him with a happy voice. Puppies are easily distracted, and he should immediately forget what he'd planned to do and come running to you. Reward him for coming and give him something more suitable to get his teeth into.
- If your puppy's got a taste for something that can't be moved – a table leg for example, spray it with a pet-friendly anti-chew, or citronella.

When will it end?

Your puppy's need to gnaw on everything in sight will
go away, but it won't be overnight. In fact, it will
probably take well over a year.

23. DIGGING

It's natural for dogs to dig. That's not to say your puppy will, because not all dogs do. But if your puppy does take too much of a liking to digging, here's something you can try.

- Find him a place where he IS allowed to dig.
- Bury things for him in that spot and let him find them.
- Then, if you find him digging in other places, tell him 'No!' or 'Leave!', fill the hole he has made back up, and show him again where he can and should dig instead.

TIP
If the problem persists, make an unpleasant
clanging noise whenever you see him starting to dig.
Hit a pot with a metal spoon for example.
Soon he'll associate digging – either in that place
or altogether – with this horrible noise.

24. BARKING

Your puppy will bark for a very good reason, no reason at all, just for fun, to make suggestions ... and sometimes even to make demands. Yes, he will have a whole box-full of bark tricks, each with their own distinct message. You will soon learn the difference between barks that are attention-seeking and those that are genuinely nervous or excited.

Barking at others

It's natural for him to warn you about intruders, or anyone he might consider as an intruder, and that kind of barking is not necessarily something you want to stop or even discourage. Let him bark at them, just momentarily, then call him back to you and praise him, or distract him with a toy or an exercise if you need to.

But if your puppy is barking at a passer-by – or the neighbour's cat, which is more likely at this stage – and you do want him to stop, your instinct is probably to shout at him to keep quiet. But put yourself in his shoes and you will see that if you shout at him while he is barking, he is likely to interpret your shouting as 'people barking', and think you are egging him on, or even coming to help. The result? He will bark even harder.

So with unwanted barking, as with pretty much all bad behaviour, it's more effective to give him the 'I'm ignoring you now!' treatment.

- Don't talk to him or touch him
- Instead look away, lift your hands away, and turn away
- Leave the room or area if you can
- If he won't stop barking and it's becoming a problem, you could distract him with a loud noise (like hitting a pot with a metal spoon)
- When he has settled down and come to you, you can acknowledge and reward him for his new-found quiet behaviour.

Barking at you

As your puppy comes to see that his efforts to win your attention, like jumping up or nipping, are fruitless, he might well replace these with his latest greatest trick – a demanding bark that says:

- I am still here
- Stop ignoring me
- Hey, I want some of that too
- Come on, let's play.

Whatever it is, he wants your attention. Don't give it to him. Instead, pull out the ignoring techniques described above.

But, as always, when he has quietened down,
be sure to acknowledge and reward him.

Incessant barking

This is seldom without reason, and the reason is all too often because he is lonely, frustrated, bored or needs attention. For example, if he is left on his own for long periods, shut in a small space or, worse still, tied up, he WILL bark incessantly. And who could blame him? In cases like this, where the barking is linked to a genuine need, it is the cause that needs to change.

Do

- Move him to a less isolated place.
- Arrange for there to be more space for him to play in.
- Take him for long or longer walks.
- Give him more time to interact with you and other dogs.
- Get another dog. Dogs are highly sociable creatures.

NEVER leave your puppy alone for a long time, never mind in a small space. As an adult, he shouldn't be left on his own for long periods either. It's simply not fair.

25. STEPPING OUT

Once your puppy has been fully vaccinated you can start walking him out and taking him on outings. But first he needs to practise walking on the lead at home, and while you're waiting for his vaccinations to take effect is the ideal time.

Eventually you want him walking by your side on a loose lead, but for a puppy, with seemingly endless stores of pent-up energy, this is surprisingly difficult to learn.

Do

- Use a normal collar (no choke chains) and a six-foot non-extendable lead.
- Attach the lead when he is calm and not resisting you.
- Start by letting him wander around the house with the lead trailing behind him, but try not to let him chew it.
- The next stage is to pick up the lead and encourage him to walk along beside you.
- If he pulls, stand still and call him to you. Praise him, then try again.
- When he is walking nicely alongside you, with the lead slack but off the ground, reward him generously with praise and treats.

Don't

- Use a choke chain or half check.
- Drag him. That would only make him panic and pull away.
- Be pulled along by him. That would teach him that pulling works in his favour.
- If he is pulling, don't pull him back to you, or yank on the lead, or shout at him. Instead, stop and call him to you and praise him for coming when he does.

When the time comes for him to get out and about, here are a few things to consider and be aware of.

Safety

Think carefully about where you're going to take him, and when, so you can avoid frightening or stressful experiences. Choose:

- a safe, open space away from busy roads,
- a place where other dog owners are likely to act in a responsible way,
- and think about the best time to go. Perhaps it's too soon for a Saturday morning at the park if there is likely to be a noisy sports match in play.

If something does scare him on an outing, let him know you are with him, protecting him, and that he is safe.

What to take

Make sure you have him on his lead (a short one is better to start with) and are armed with:

- Biodegradable poo bags – more than one
- Treats (ideally in a treat pouch) – so you can reward good behaviour

- Water and a bowl – if there is no clean water where you are going. (As a space saver, you might like to invest in a pets' water bottle with a flap or lid that doubles as a bowl.)

Pooping

If he poops, pick it up with a poo bag and dispose of it at home (or in a public dog waste bin if one is provided).

Other dogs

When you come across other dogs on your outings, you could use the opportunity for your puppy to practise his meeting and greeting. But never assume that other people or their dogs are happy to reciprocate. And never let your dog run up to other dogs unless their walkers have told you it's okay. There are lots of reasons why it might not be. Perhaps the dog is very old; maybe it is injured; in recovery; not good with puppies; or the owner is working on a specific training exercise. Always ask first and from a distance:

1. whether their dog is good with puppies and
2. whether they are happy for your puppy to say 'hello'.

If it is okay for your dogs to meet, stay close by to supervise, and to pre-empt any bad experiences.

Make sure you walk on past some dogs, and people too, so your puppy doesn't take it for granted that he can run up to anyone for a chin- and tail-wag.

Play dates

If your puppy meets another dog he plays especially well with, you could arrange play dates at times that suit you both.

Together time

- Put your smart phone out of temptation's way and make this quality time with your puppy!
- If you are going somewhere with big open spaces like the park, you can take a long, extendable lead. But NEVER pull your puppy back with the line. He should come to you as called. There is more on this in 'Training'.

26. EXERCISE

Exercise helps to keep your dog trim, healthy and happy, and prevents boredom, unruly behaviour and weight gain. And that goes for us owners too. It's truly a win-win.

Between eight and eleven weeks of age, your puppy needs two to three walks a day of no more than 10-15 minutes at a time.

From 12 weeks (three months), start adding five minutes to the length of each walk per month, so that by four months, his walks are approximately 20 minutes each; by five months, they last around 25 minutes, and so on.

As a rule, more shorter walks are better for puppies than fewer longer ones.

As an adult, your dog will need an hour or two of exercise a day, depending on how active he is, and it's up to you to find ways to give him the exercise he needs.

Walking

Walking is fantastic, low-impact exercise for you both. Once your puppy is walking nicely on the lead, you can start picking up the pace, gradually working up to a brisker walk and over longer distances.

Running

Never jog with your puppy, because his bones are still forming. If you decide to start running with him when he is fully-grown then, as with the walking, work up the distances slowly. You would also need to be mindful of his paws because dogs aren't well booted like you. Stay away from long stretches of hard ground and be aware of surfaces that might be very hot, or cold and icy.

Some dogs make better running partners than others: Pointers, Collies and German Shepherds are a few examples of the bigger breeds that have the build, stamina and inclination to make good partners; and Jack Russells are a good example of a smaller breed. Many mixed breed dogs make excellent running partners too, because they are less likely than many purebreds to develop genetic disorders.

NOTE
Never jog or run with your dog of any age if it is a Brachycephaly (a flat-faced breed) because of respiratory problems.

Swimming

Some dogs love to swim, and take to the water like ducks. Typical examples are Retrievers, Standard Poodles, Newfoundlands, Setters and the Irish Water

Spaniels. But whatever your puppy's mix or breed, if he grows into a swimmer, this is an excellent, low-impact exercise, and can be particularly good for dogs that suffer from joint problems in later life.

But don't force your dog to swim (or push him into anything he doesn't want to do). That said, if he needs to learn for safety reasons, start him somewhere with a gradual incline into the water, or at the shallowest step of a pool. (See **Swimming pools and deep water** in the chapter 'Danger Alert!'.) Go in with him and ease him in. He might try to walk on the water at first, lifting his front feet right out with each step. If he does this, hold his bottom up so that his front feet stay underwater, while also supporting him under his ribcage.

If he walks in on his own, then stops before he loses contact with the bottom, you could support him under his ribcage, keeping him level until he gets the hang of it.

Games and playtime

These also count towards his daily exercise and are especially fantastic for mental stimulation. The chapter 'Playtime' is filled with ideas and tips.

BUT

All of these activities come with their own risks – some obvious and others totally unpredictable, so here is a shortlist of things to be acutely aware of. It is not meant to discourage you from taking him into the great outdoors or giving him the exercise he absolutely must have; it's just to help you avoid taking chances with his safety.

On land:

- Even if your puppy or dog is hugely reliable off the lead, blind trust is still careless. Don't let him loose anywhere near traffic – dogs can cover a lot of ground very quickly and squirrels, rabbits and deer for example could lure him on a merry chase.
- Make sure you know the area well before letting him off the lead – apart from roadways, be aware of cliffs, drainage culverts and thin ice.
- Although your dog might feel invincible on a walk, some animals will get the better of him. As far as possible, keep him away from snakes, porcupines and skunks.
- Be careful not to let him graze on greenery on hikes. Not all tasty plants are agreeable, or even safe.
- If he's walking along the coast, keep him away from dead fish.
- If you come across cattle grazing, give them a wide berth and don't let your puppy or dog run after them.

In water:

As a basic rule, whether he is swimming intentionally or just happens to be near open water, take the same precautions with him as you would with a young child.

- Very cold water can cause hypothermia, which could drain him of his strength to swim to land.
- In the sea, stay clear of rough waves, undertows and side currents.
- Rivers are dangerous when they are fast-flowing, eddying or moving towards a waterfall or weir.

- Be especially careful of steep banks – natural drops as well as manmade ones on the edges of ditches and canals. Anything he could not easily get out of.
- If it's a swimming pool he's in, make sure he knows where the step is and how to get out.
- In the wild, consider the possibility of other animals in the water: alligators, crocs, sharks, snapping turtles.

27. TRAINING

'Properly trained, a man can be dog's best friend'
Corey Ford

You most likely assume that puppy training is about training your puppy – most people do – but in actual fact it is nearly all about you, the owner, learning how to communicate effectively with your puppy.

And puppy training is not all about tricks either. It is about mutual understanding that naturally results in basic obedience and a better quality of life for you, your puppy … and everyone he meets.

Everything from the chapter 'Behaviour' applies to this chapter too because the premise for training is the same: encourage and reward good behaviour. Always tell your puppy what you DO want him to do, rather than what you DON'T want him to do, because he will be more engaged when he has nothing to fear.

And training should be fun. The best trained dogs wag their tails during training because they enjoy the challenge as well as the reward.

Reward-based training

Praise is always a motivator in training but it is often not enough, so using food as the key incentive, at least at first, has become commonly accepted. Use small treats to get you started, keeping praise as a secondary reinforcer. In time you will be able to wean your dog from the food-based training, and he will obey you purely for the fun of the training itself. But even then, you should reward him with treats intermittently.

When to start

Training starts the moment you bring your puppy home. Even if you've signed up for puppy classes at some future date, don't wait. Teach him what you can, little by little, moment by moment. Practise often, and never give up. (It's worth mentioning here that while it is never too early to start training, it is also never too late.)

Who's responsible

Anyone and everyone in your puppy's close and extended family.

Where?

Start training in a quiet place with no outside distractions. A closed room is infinitely better than a park with other puppies play-fighting nearby.

What?

By the time he is six months old, your puppy should know his name and obey your orders to: 'Come', 'Sit' and 'Down'. He should also have been introduced to 'Stay'.

How?

Use the spoken commands, hand signals and body language that you agreed on as a family.

All verbal commands should be spoken clearly, firmly and with confidence. At least initially, lengthen the vowel sounds and make sure the consonants are crisp and clear.

Your voice and treats are key to training your puppy, but don't forget about gestures. It might surprise you to learn that most dogs respond better to body language than to words.

NAME RECOGNITION

One of the first things your puppy needs to learn is to recognise his name. This is how he will know when you're communicating specifically with him.

Do

- From a short distance – three or four feet is fine – call your puppy clearly, using his name just once.
- Use a happy, friendly voice.
- Crouch down if you can.

- Open your arms to welcome him (body language is hugely important).
- Make a fuss of him when he gets to you.
- If he doesn't respond, wait a few seconds then call again, still clearly, and still just the once.
- When he does come, praise him lovingly, give him a small treat and tell him how brilliantly clever he is.
- Practise this often.

Don't

- Overuse his name or say it repeatedly in quick succession, or he will soon learn to ignore it.

EYE CONTACT

If your puppy is not looking at you, he is probably not listening either. Calling his name will encourage him to look at you and, when he does, you can know he's engaged. He's turning to you to find out what's coming next: will you open the door, take him for a walk, throw the ball? It's excellent that he's turning to you for answers and provision, so make sure you reward him.

CALLING HIM TO YOU

If your dog only knows one command it should be 'Come' or 'Here'. Coming to you when he's called is important for your relationship, and essential for his safety too. Recall is much like the name recognition exercise and now, while he is little, is a very good time to teach it to him because this is when he needs you more than ever for love, food and safety. In fact, if he's already joined your family, chances are he is with you right now, under your feet or helping you to absorb this book. Digest it even. And chances are he already relates the recall command to something fun and exciting: food, a new toy or play time.

Do

- Follow the steps in the Name Recognition exercise above, using his name and adding a calling word like 'Come' or 'Here'. Consistency is key, so choose which word you prefer and stick with it.
- Call him to you often, gradually increasing the initial distance between you.
- Practise at home and on a lead before you let him go when you are out and about.
- When you do let him off the lead away from home, make sure it is in a very safe place. Then practise letting him go and calling him back.
- If he keeps following you anyway, find someone who can help you by holding him while you back away. Then entice him, if necessary, and when he is struggling to get to you, your helper can let him go. Only then, when he is running to you, call his name, adding 'Come' or 'Here'.
- Your welcoming body language can be very helpful with this too. Try getting down on your haunches or your knees and opening your arms wide to greet him.

Don't

- If you call your dog to you and he gets side-tracked en route, you might be tempted to scold him when he finally arrives. But coming to you should **always** be associated with good things, so never punish him if he doesn't come straight away. If you do, he'll associate the scolding with the last thing he's done – come to you. Then, understandably from his point of view, he'll think twice the next time about coming back at all. (See 'Timing is all-important' in the chapter on Behaviour.)

- Don't put him back on the lead every time he comes to you, or he will soon learn that coming means the end of his free-play session. Only put him back on after several recalls.

TIP

If he develops the habit of running up to you but then dancing around just out of your reach, start withholding his treat until AFTER you have a grip on his collar

'SIT'

This is one of the most useful exercises you can teach your puppy.

- Call him to you and hold a treat, palm facing down, just in front of his nose for him to smell.
- When you've got his interest, slowly take the treat up a couple of inches and over his head (slightly behind and above his eyes).

- When he lowers his bottom, say 'Sit!' and give him the treat.
- Once he is doing this well, you can move on to the next stage. Wait until his bottom is actually on the floor before you say 'Sit!', and only then give him the treat.
- He will soon learn to associate the word with the action. In time you can teach him to sit for longer stretches, from further away and during distractions.

NOTE
Be careful not to ask him to 'Sit down!' if you only want him to 'Sit!', because once he has learned the 'Down!' command as well, he won't know whether you're asking for a 'Sit' or a 'Down'

'DOWN'

- It is best to start teaching this command when your puppy is already in an attentive sit.
- Without feeding him the treat in your hand, move your hand, still palm down, from above his nose and towards the floor, between his front paws and close to his body.
- When he lowers his nose and front paws, keeping his bottom on the ground, say 'Down!' in a clear voice and give him the treat.
- When he is doing this well, you can wait until his tummy and all four paws are flat on the floor before you say 'Down!', and only then give him the treat.

NOTE

You need to be careful with this command too – not to use it when he is on a piece of furniture he is not meant to be on. If you shout 'Down!' at him to get down off the sofa and he is already 'lying down', you will just confuse him. Rather say 'Off!'

'STAY'

This is an essential command for the safety or your puppy – or any dog that would otherwise dash out the front door, across a road, or leap out of the car.

The training involves teaching him to remain in a Sit or Down position for increasingly long times before you reward him.

- Once he is in a 'Sit' or a 'Down', say 'Stay!' in a strong but soothing voice, and combine this with a clear hand signal. With your arm straight, your palm flat and your fingers together, point to the ground just in front of him.
- If he gets up, simply ask for the Sit or Down position again and repeat the 'Stay' command.
- When he has stayed for a few seconds, say 'Good!' (or another 'release' word of your choice) and give him a treat.
- Gradually work up to longer times, but no more than 30 seconds, and step back in increments to increase the distance. (There's no point giving him unrealistic goals, so the idea is to push him to the limit while letting him succeed.)
- Keep him on a lead when you put this command into practice at the front door or in the car.

What if the training's 'not working'?

If your puppy doesn't do what you've asked (assuming he's not hard of hearing):

- he doesn't understand and needs clearer instructions,
- or he needs more practice,
- or he needs a better reason to obey you – like a treat, an even better treat, or higher praise.

EXPANDING ON THE BASICS

Extension exercises

Duration – Once your puppy can do an exercise, like 'Sit' for example, you can gradually ask him to sit for longer periods before treating him.

Distractions – You can slowly increase the distractions too. A 'Sit' in a quiet place is very different from a 'Sit' when a squirrel is taunting your puppy from a nearby tree. Once he's mastered the instruction in a quiet room, start practising it in a busier part of the house, then at the park, then on a street corner, and so on.

Distance – In time, you can also begin asking your puppy to 'Sit' from slightly further away from you, but start with just a couple of steps and don't forget the all-important hand signals.

Advanced commands – If you'd like to add to these basic commands, your puppy can go on to learn 'Stand', 'Settle', 'Heel' and many more. There are some excellent obedience training books on the market, and if training classes are available in your area, they are well worth the effort and your dog would love you for taking him.

28. PLAYTIME

Playing with your puppy helps to develop his socialising, improve his communication skills, and give him the mental and physical exercise he needs. Most importantly of all, it's great fun. But whether you're just messing around or trying something more structured, you should always keep these Rules of Play top of mind.

- Start playtimes when your puppy's being good, so you're not rewarding him for bad behaviour.
- Several short play sessions spread throughout the day are always better than one long one.
- Whatever games you're playing, remember he's only little, so don't overpower him. Be sure to match your strength, speed and energy to his own.
- As far as possible, get down low to his level (small children excepted).
- If a toy is involved, avoid hard tugging. Never let his feet leave the ground as he clings to a toy. It puts too much pressure on his teeth, and encourages more aggressive play. Holding the toy by your fingertips is a good way to manage the pressure.
- When your puppy wins the toy, encourage him back to teach him that playing is more about having fun together than possession.
- If the playing does shift from fun interaction to possession of a toy, then stop for a while.
- Always try to calm the playing down before you

stop. It's disappointing stopping a game when it's at its most exciting.

- And always end playtime on a good note. If you've had to stop for a moment, restart the game and end it when things are quiet and friendly.

For playtime to be great fun, you just need each other – there's no need for fancy toys or expensive equipment. Sharing a walk, throwing a ball and paddling in the shallows can be the most special of times. But if you're still looking to expand your activities and make your time together even more enriching, here are some ideas.

GAMES

All puppies have their favourites and you will soon figure out which ones you play best together.

Chase

This game is excellent practice for encouraging your puppy to come to you when he is older.

1. Flick a treat across the floor.
2. Let him chase after it.
3. When he comes back for more, make eye contact and praise him.
4. Only then flick another treat across the floor, and so on.

Fetch

This is an extension of Chase, but outside or in a much bigger space.

1. Throw things for him to fetch: toys, a ball, a treat.
2. Say 'Fetch!' as you throw each item.
3. Once he knows to fetch, start throwing the objects into harder-to-reach places.
4. If this doesn't work, throw more interesting toys or tastier treats.

Catch

You can play this with toys, treats and balls.

1. Start with something light and easy to grab hold of, like a floppy soft toy.
2. Throw it in an arc over his head, so that if he stayed in place it would land close to his muzzle.
3. If he misses, try to pick it up before him and he will soon learn that if he wants it he must catch it before it hits the ground.
4. When he's learned to catch, you can move on to balls as well. (Much later he can progress to frisbees which are even more challenging, but be sure to start with a soft disc.)

Which hand?

1. With your hands behind your back, put a small treat or two in one hand and nothing in the other.
2. Make your hands into fists and bring them in front of you.
3. Let your puppy choose which fist he prefers the smell of.
4. When he's decided which hand he's interested in, and it's the right one, say 'Good!' and open your hand, letting him take the treat.

Treasure hunt

This is all about sniffing things out and your puppy will love it! What's more, rooting around for hidden treasure can be played just as well indoors as out.

1. The first time you play, let him follow you and watch as you hide a treat (something he can eat), then lead him away and say 'Find'.

2. As a next step, you could ask someone to hold him while he watches you hide the treat. When you get back to him, you can let him 'Find'.

3. Once he understands how the game works, you can make sure he can't see you at all when you hide the treat or a toy. Then lead him into the room or area of the garden where it's hidden, say 'Find', and this time he will have to follow your smell. (The first few times you might need to guide him.)

One day, when he is older, well trained and fully understands the game, you can make it more difficult by using 'Sit!' and 'Stay!' while you hide the treat, and then start hiding it in more difficult places too.

The memory game

When your puppy is a little older and has mastered some easy games, you can move on to more difficult challenges, like this one.

1. Put a treat in a sealed box or bag (because we want him to remember where it is rather than sniffing it out) and let him watch while you hide it.

2. Lead him away and distract him (for no more than 30 seconds at first).

3. Then say 'Where is it?', and initially you might need to guide him.

4. When he understands how the game works, you can make the distraction time longer and longer.

Obstacle course

1. Turn your passageway or garden into an obstacle course – build jumps, make tunnels, fill a tea tray with water, arrange boxes to navigate around … anything you can think of that is safe.
2. Guide your puppy through the course and reward him with treats each time he overcomes an obstacle.

TOYS

To keep your puppy interested in his toys, don't put them all out at the same time. Only let him play with or chew a few at a time, and rotate them during the day or through the week.

Presumably he'll have a range of toys that roll, bounce or squeak – toys that are wonderfully chewy or simply soft and cuddly. But here are three ideas for playtime that are a little more interesting and challenging.

The maze

There are a number of 'slow feeder' pet toys on the market which are maze-like in design. They are intended for dogs who gulp their food down too fast, but they also work brilliantly for brain-training.

- Put a treat or two in the middle and let him use his paws, snout and tongue to work the treats out of the maze before he can eat them.

The hollow chew

Hollow toys made of hard rubber, the Kong for

example, are available online and from most pet stores. Fill one of these with small dog treats, or even with peanut butter (as long as it contains no Xylitol), or marmite if you can get hold of it. Your dog will spend hours trying to crunch or lick out whatever you've filled it up with.

Activity balls

There are plenty of these on the market in a range of shapes and sizes. Put dry food or treats inside one of these and your puppy will love rolling it around to get the pieces out.

EQUIPMENT

Use your imagination, but make sure whatever you come up with is safe, and well secured where necessary.

- Hay bales can be used as jumps, steps and passageways
- Old tires make fabulous jump hoops
- Children's paddling pools are great fun for playing in as well as cooling off in on hot days
- Look in children's toy stores – tunnels, playhouses and sand boxes will all appeal to your puppy too.

29. TRAVELLING BY CAR

Of course your puppy would love nothing more than to stand on the front passenger seat, stick his head out the window and feel the wind in his face, but car travel is not the time for free play.

Ideally you should invest in one of the following, depending on whether you want your dog to travel on the back seats, or – if your car has a rear door – in the space behind the back seats.

- a seatbelt harness – well-padded and comfortable, that fastens securely into your vehicle's existing seatbelt fitting,
- a crate or cage that is small enough to fit in the back area of your car while also being big enough for your adult dog to sit up and have a stretch in,
- a dog guard – fitted between the back seats of your car and the trunk/boot area.

All of these are available in pet stores and online.

Do

- Whenever you are getting your dog into the car or letting him out, make sure it is on the pavement side of the road.
- For everyone's safety, use a doggy seatbelt, crate or cage, or dog guard.
- For his own safety, teach him to 'Stay!' in the car until he is given the command to exit.

- On long journeys, stop regularly to let him relieve himself and stretch his legs. These stops will also help ease any car sickness he might experience.

Never

- Get him into or out of the car on the traffic side of the road.
- Allow your puppy or dog on your lap while you're driving.
- Allow him on the front passenger seat, especially if an airbag is fitted.
- Tie him in place on the back seat by his collar and lead instead of using a proper seatbelt harness.
- Leave him strapped into the car in the blaring sunlight. This would hurt him just as much as it would you.
- Leave him unattended in a hot or even warm car for more than five minutes. If you do **have** to leave him for a few minutes, make sure at least one of the windows is open a couple of centimetres, or more if it's safe. Dog fatalities from heatstroke in cars are frighteningly common.

30. PUPPY-PEOPLE TRANSLATOR

Your dog understands your every word, or so it's said. The point is, your choice of words is very important. Even more important though is how you say them. Be clear in your body language and be gentle but firm, patient, loving, encouraging, reassuring.

It is also said that a dog can say more with his tail in just a few seconds than his owner can say in hours. If he's already in your life, you will be familiar with his favourite expressions: 'I am so happy to see you!' and 'You are the best thing that ever happened to me!' In his earliest days with you, you will no doubt have braced yourself for, 'Your face is like a lovely lolly!' And before long – but only if you've been 'good' – you could be surprised by another frequent favourite: 'Your training is coming along very nicely.'

Yup, a lot of your puppy's body language is really easy to read, but truth be told the signs are not always straightforward. How good are you really at understanding his language? By way of example, a wagging tail can be a sign of happiness as well as one of aggression, so you really do need to look at the whole picture including: how he wags it, what the rest of his body is doing at the time and what else is going on around him.

To help with this, here are some people–puppy translations:

I love you - Racing to meet you
- Wagging tail
- Licking
- Whimpering

**I'm happy
and excited** - Tail wagging fast (but watch out as this can also be a sign of concentration or aggression)
- Racing around
- Whimpering
- Pulling lips back and exposing teeth

Let's play - Wagging tail vigorously
- Rolling head
- Dashing off and jumping back again
- Jumping in front of you, facing you, front legs splayed out
- Elbows on the ground and bottom in the air (the play-bow)

What is that sound? Where is it coming from?	- Bounding leaps - Running in circles - Lying down or rolling over - Barking intermingled with growls (can be confused with aggression) - One paw raised - Head tilted to the side - Brow raised - Ears twitching and nose wiggling - Mouth may be open and panting
Totally chilled out	- Lying on back with legs flopped out - Curled in a ball - Lying down watching you
Feeling submissive	- Rolling over onto back, exposing tummy and genitals - Tail between legs - Head dipped or tucked in, ears pinned back
I'm curious, and maybe a little concerned, about something going on out there	- Raised paw

I'm frightened or unhappy
- Tail between legs
- Cowering, or lying down
- Ears twitching back and forth
- Staring ahead at object of fear
- Lying down with paws ahead, looking ahead, ready to run
- Raised hackles (hairs along the top of his back)
- Whining
- Whimpering
- Looking to you for help

I'm in pain or frightened and want your help
- Looking from you to whatever it is he needs, and then quickly back again
- Whining or whimpering
  This is not manipulation. It's a genuine plea for help. Tell him you're there for him and he can count on you.

Aggressive
- Standing up straight
- Ears pinned back, or sharply forward
- Raised hackles
- Low growl with eyes fixed in a direct stare
- Body is tense, ready to attack
- Tail held stiffly, or wagging in stiff, quick, stilted movements
- Barking

- Sudden unpredictable bites
- Growling or biting (in attack, but can also be in response to punishment, or in defence of food or toys)

I'm warning you
- Snarling
- Growling
- Baring fangs

Feeling lonely and locating other dogs, or sending out a warning
- Howling
- Baying

I want your attention: 'hello', 'look at me', 'I'm bored'
- Barking directly at you

I'm begging you. Pleeez!
- Whining, with pleading eyes
  Yes, it's a heart-wrenching expression, but don't give in to that adorable face. Your environment will help you to tell the difference between manipulative begging and 'I'm in pain or frightened and need your help'. If you're eating a juicy steak that he's hoping you'll share, it's safe to assume he's begging.

31. ADOLESCENCE

Somewhere between four and 20 months your puppy will go through adolescence (yes, the timing is that vague).

This is usually the most difficult period for owners. He is growing in independence; his chewing continues relentlessly; and he will become more territorial. Hopefully the solid foundations you've laid in the early weeks and months will make this stage a little less wearing.

Remind yourself it is short-lived.

Running off

If your adolescent puppy starts running off, and this behaviour persists, prevention is always the better option. At home you will need to keep him inside or in a fully-enclosed garden or yard, and while walking out he will need to stay on the lead.

But if he does run off (or away), be sure to praise him when he comes back (or home). Never scold him when he gets to you, because in coming back he is being a good puppy. That way he will want to stay with you (or home) and, even if he does run off again, he will always want to return.

Sexual maturity

If your puppy does start trying to run off, it's most likely because around this time – typically six to nine months (or later with the largest breeds) – he or she will be at the onset of sexual maturity. Females will come into season and be overcome with the urge to roam, and males could begin mounting things, marking their territory and maybe even fighting with other male dogs. Both sexes will experience hormonal changes that are likely to affect their behaviour, so if you're not considering breeding, you will soon be faced with making the important decision of whether or not to have your dog neutered (spayed or castrated).

NEUTERING

To neuter or not to neuter? This highly controversial subject is beyond the parameters of this book, so suffice it to say here that most vets and breeders consider neutering the more responsible option. Here are some of the key pros and cons.

Neutering your female dog

(also referred to as spaying or de-sexing)

Advantages:

- prevents unwanted pregnancies
- stops her from coming into season (also referred to as coming into heat), which involves bleeding for two to four weeks at a time, approximately every six to eight months.
- stops her from trying to escape to find a mate
- keeps persistent male dogs from pursuing her
- reduces the risk of a number of health problems, including infections of the uterus.

Disadvantages:

- It involves major surgery
- It increases the risk of obesity
- It increases the risk of a number of health problems, especially if done too early.

Neutering your male dog

(also referred to as castrating or de-sexing)

Advantages:

- prevents accidental breeding
- lessens dominance and aggression
- cuts back on undesirable sexual behaviour
- reduces leg lifting and urine marking
- lowers the urge to run off after females in season
- minimises the risk of his being attacked by other males
- reduces the risk of a number of health problems, including prostate disorders and testicular cancer.

Disadvantages:

- It involves major surgery
- It increases the risk of obesity
- It increases the risk of a number of health problems, especially if done too early.

When to neuter

This is a hugely important consideration, because neutering too early can result in emotional and behavioural problems as well as some serious health issues. Emotionally for example, it can be linked to increased fear and reduced confidence. Physically, it can cause the bones to develop unevenly; as well as increase the risk of obesity and bone cancer, and in females, urinary incontinence. The bottom line is that you shouldn't have your puppy neutered too soon, even though waiting is likely to cause some inconvenience to you in the short term.

But the safest and most sensible timing is also debatable because it varies not just from breed to breed but also from dog to dog. Ideally this is when your puppy/dog has reached physical as well as emotional maturity.

Physical maturity

As a very rough guide:

- The average small dog *(Dachshund, Maltese, Chihuahua)* – having an adult weight of up to 11kg (25lb) – will reach its full adult frame size between 10 and 12 months.
- The average medium-sized dog *(Miniature Schnauzer, Cocker Spaniel, Beagle)* – weighing 11-23kg (25-50lb) as an adult – will reach its full

adult frame size between 12 and 15 months.

- The average large-breed dog *(Boxer, Pit Bull, Golden Retriever)* – weighing over 23kg (50lb) as an adult – won't reach its full adult frame size until around 18 months, but the largest breeds can continue filling out and gaining muscle until they are two or even three years of age.

If you know your dog's breed, or a close comparison if he's a mix, it is well worth doing some breed-specific research, even before visiting the vet. A responsible vet will never encourage early neutering without very good reason.

Emotional maturity

When your dog reaches emotional maturity is more difficult to pinpoint, and yet just as important for his wellbeing. Good indicators are:

- less bounce and
- reduced chewing.

NOTE

Neutering won't automatically solve all your puppy issues completely, or overnight, but it should help improve bad behaviour in time

32. GOING FORWARD

Fear period

As if adolescence isn't tricky enough, between seven and eight months of age your puppy could also experience another fear period, so you do need to be especially gentle and understanding around then.

The special place

When your puppy is toilet trained and has stopped eating everything in sight, you will be able to start leaving the door to his crate or special space open. In the meantime, remember to keep praising him when you see him going in there on his own.

Feeding

It is your job to manage your puppy's food intake and keep a check on his weight. Extra weight puts unnecessary strain on his joints and organs, so keep treats to a minimum.

Between five months and a year old you will also be able to cut his feeds back from three times to twice a day.

At around a year you can move him on from puppy to adult food. And remember that if he shows signs of a food allergy – by scratching, licking or chewing his legs or paws, or rubbing his face – switching to a low-grain or grain-free diet can help to alleviate the symptoms. If his food bowls are plastic, switching to stainless steel or ceramic has also been said to make a difference.

Throughout your dog's life, his weight needs to be controlled by a sensible diet together with sufficient exercise, and this is especially important if he or she has been neutered.

Nails

Apart from being uncomfortable, nails that are too long can cause splayed feet and lameness. Some dogs never need their nails clipped, but most do. You can tell that your dog's nails need a trim:

- if his toes splay apart,
- if his nails scratch the ground when he's standing upright,
- or if you can hear them clacking on the floor.

Not all dogs have dewclaws – the nails higher up on the insides of the legs – but if yours does, these will need trimming too to prevent them from catching on things or growing into the skin. Some owners used to have their dog's dewclaws surgically removed, but nowadays, unless they are malformed or causing discomfort, the practice is compared to chopping off a person's thumb.

Past the puppy stage

This book has set out to answer the most important early-stage questions for new puppy parents. But this is just the beginning of a lifelong journey with your new family member. Going forward, you might well choose to fine-tune your training, or need to deal with specific behavioural issues that could've arisen. There are some excellent and extremely thorough books on the market. And if you've got the time and inclination for obedience training classes, they are incredibly enriching for both you and your dog. He would love you for taking him, forever and more.

33. THERE WILL BE TIMES ...

This book is intended as an easy read to offer you some shortcuts with the theory. But there are NO shortcuts with the practice. The practice needs patience and repetition, encouragement and reward.

Tough times

There will be times when your puppy does all sorts of things you don't want him to. When he's bored and teething, he will set his alligator jaws to work, chomping their happy way through your designer chairs. He will gift you with shredded items of now ex-value, and random deposits of unidentifiable bodily waste.

He will slop his muddy paws across your cream-coloured carpet, then wait until he's well and truly indoors before shaking himself off. He will bark when he has something to say, and whine when he's upset or lonely.

For months, your house will be littered with toys, and the pitter-patter of determined paws will be under your feet when you go to the fridge, the toilet, the shower and the front door.

There will be many times when you're at your wits' end and you look at him and think, 'What **have** I got myself into?'

Well it's this: you have a new family member who

will bowl you over with his love and affection. If he's a shedder, he will distribute his coat generously, far and wide. If he's big, he will take up space on your bed, sofa, passage floor and/or entrance area – in fact, wherever he is allowed you will be navigating your way around him. If he's high-energy, he will need so much exercise that you'll struggle to keep up. If he's protective, he will bark at strangers, and decide who should be allowed to visit you. If he's just straight gorgeous, he will have you wrapped around his little paw-kins. And if you aren't firm enough with the rules, your new family member will soon be ruling the house.

But it's precisely because of these enriching, sometimes-frustrating qualities that we love them so much. So remember this when you feel your patience running thin.

And no matter how often he seems to you like a small child covered in fur, don't try to make him more human. Just as he is, you will have more love and more fun than you could ever imagine, and there will be many times when you ask yourself, 'How did I get so lucky?'

Good times

Your family has grown by four furry feet and when you get home, that wet nose, wiggling bottom and wagging tail wait to greet you. He will melt your heart with his loyalty, gratitude, forgiveness and protection. He will enrich your life with his unconditional love, and bring you buckets of laughs with his bumbling antics.

There will also be plenty of times when he does the things you DO want him to do. Praise him – with attention, treats, toys … it doesn't matter what, as long as it's something he loves.

Taking-him-for-granted times

And last, but definitely not least, there will be times when he just IS – a calm, quiet presence by your side. Those are the times when it will be easiest for you to forget or ignore him, and those are the times when it is most important of all to remind yourself, and him, just how special he is.

34. USEFUL CONTACTS

WEBSITES

American Kennel Club
www.akc.org

Australian National Kennel Council
ankc.org.au

Canadian Kennel Club
www.kck.ca/en

Company of Animals
CompanyofAnimals.co.uk

Dogs New Zealand
www.dogsnz.org.nz

KUSA (Kennel Union of Southern Africa)
www.kusa.co.za

The Kennel Club (UK)
www.thekennelclub.org.uk

The Dog Training Secret
thedogtrainingsecret.com

United Kennel Club
The world's largest all-breed registry for performance dogs
www.ukcdogs.com

Rescue, Adoption and Re-homing Centres
There are far too many to mention here, but a quick internet search should bring up the options in your area.

INDEX

Printed in Great Britain
by Amazon